FAITH
FOR THE
FEARFUL?

An investigation into new churches
in the greater Durban area

E.S. Morran
L. Schlemmer

Commissioned by DIAKONIA on behalf
of its member churches

CENTRE FOR APPLIED SOCIAL SCIENCES
UNIVERSITY OF NATAL   DURBAN
August 1984

ISBN   0 86980 396 4

PREFACE AND ACKNOWLEDGEMENTS

This study of new churches was commissioned by Diakonia,
a joint project of established churches in the greater Durban area, the
basic aim of which is to mobilise member churches for social action.
Diakonia's interest in and concern about the new churches arose principally because the new churches appear to be discouraging their members
from developing an interest in issues of social justice.   The role of
the new churches might be counterproductive for the progress of justice
and peace in South Africa.

In addition the rapid growth of the new churches might to some extent
reflect on the established churches' ability to address the needs of
followers, and it was thought that a thorough investigation of the new
churches would provide valuable lessons and insights for the established
churches in how to cope with the challenges posed by divergent needs
in congregations.

In order to ensure that the terms used in this study are uniformly
understood a brief explanation of the most common terms used is
provided on page (iii).   In addition a glossary of additional
terminology is provided in Appendix 2.   Unless otherwise stated
Biblical quotations are taken from "The Holy Bible - King James
version".

The authors gratefully acknowledge the assitance given by the following
people: the late Professor Trevor Verryn of UNISA, John Warden
previously of the Ecumenical Research Unit (Pretoria), Neville Heuer
of the University of Durban-Westville, members of Diakonia, the
many clergymen of established churches and pastors of the new churches
who willingly gave us their opinions and insights, and the respondents
who were prepared to give in-depth answers to often very personal
questions.

The authors also wish to thank Alison Sampson and Chris Albertyn for
their comments and assistance in the tedious task of editing, and
Penny Geerdts for conducting interviews.

(iv)

PREFACE AND ACKNOWLEDGEMENTS

This study of new churches was commissioned by Diakonia,
a joint project of established churches in the greater Durban area, the
basic aim of which is to mobilise member churches for social action.
Diakonia's interest is not concern about the new churches is due principally because the new churches appear to be discouraging their members
from developing an interest in issues of social justice. The role of
the new churches might be counterproductive for the interests of justice
and peace in South Africa.

In addition the rapid growth of the new churches might to some extent
reflect on the established churches' ability to address the needs of
followers, and it was thought that a thorough investigation of the new
churches would provide valuable lessons and insights for the established
churches in how to cope with the challenge posed by burgeoning needs
in congregations.

In order to ensure that the terms used in this study are uniformly
understood, a brief explanation of the more common terms used is
provided on page (iii). In addition, a glossary of additional
terminology is provided in Appendix 2. Unless otherwise stated
Biblical quotations are taken from "The Holy Bible - King James
version".

The authors acknowledge the assistance given by the following
people: the late Professor Trevor Verryn of UNISA, John Wender
previously of the Ecumenical Research Unit (Pretoria), Neville Hewer
of the University of Durban-Westville, members of Diakonia, the
many clergymen of established churches and pastors of the new churches
who willingly gave us their opinions and insights, and the respondents
who were prepared to give in-depth answers to often very personal
questions.

The authors also wish to thank Alison Sampson and Chris Abberley for
their comments and assistance in the tedious task of editing, and
Penny Beerata for conducting interviews.

Thanks also go to all the members of the Centre for Applied Social Sciences staff who so efficiently contributed toward the production of this study: Patsy Wickham for administrative tasks, Nicolette Wells and Lynn Davies for the typing of the manuscript, and Ulla Bulteel for the data processing.

Elda Morran
Lawrence Schlemmer

Centre for Applied Social Sciences
University of Natal
DURBAN

August 1984

TERMINOLOGY

The terminology used to describe various manifestations in the area
of religion is multifarious and often confusing.   To avoid confusion
terms consistently used in this report denote the following:

New churches: this term is used to denote independent
'non-denominational' churches which
have emerged in South Africa in the
last 10 years and which, in addition to
being charismatic, propound, as a central
tenet of their teachings, the so-called
prosperity message.   Rhema churches
and Christian Centres are hence referred
to as new churches.

Charismatics: this term will be used to denote all
people who consider themselves to be
'born-again'; who have undergone a
definitive salvational experience and
who consider the infilling by the Holy
Spirit and the gifts of the Holy Spirit
to be fundamental to their belief.   In
this sense the term refers to members
of the new churches, neopentecostals
and Pentecostals.

New church charismatics:
(NCC's)   this term is used in the report to
describe adherents or members of the
new churches.

Established churches: this term is used to distinguish 'older'
more established denominations, whatever
their doctrines, from new churches.

Established church charismatics (ECC's):	this term is used to denote members of established churches who are charismatics. For the purposes of this report, neopentecostals and Pentecostals (see below) are referred to as established church charismatics.
Pentecostals:	the term is used here to refer to charismatic Christians in separate or distinct established Pentecostal denominations like the Full Gospel church and Assemblies of God.
Neopentecostals:	the term denotes charismatic Christians who have remained within non-Pentecostal denominations, e.g. Anglican charismatics, Roman Catholic charismatics, Methodist charismatics.
Mainline churches:	the term is used in this report to denote mainstream orthodox Christian churches such as Roman Catholic, Anglican, Methodist and Presbyterian churches.
Mainline church traditionalists (MCT's):	this term refers to members of mainline churches who are not charismatic. The term 'traditionalist' does not imply a value judgement but is simply used to distinguish non-charismatic Christians from charismatic Christians.

A glossary of other terms used in this report is provided in Appendix 2, p. 197.

TABLE OF CONTENTS

TABLE OF CONTENTS

(vii)

LIST OF TABLES

CHAPTER 1

INTRODUCTION

Independent, non-denominational churches have become a powerful and rapidly growing movement within Christianity in South Africa today. The Rhema churches and various Christian Centres are typical examples of these new churches. They are sufficiently and notably different from the charismatic revival in general, of which they form a part, and from their Pentecostal and evangelical roots, to warrant specific investigation. They have undoubtedly had an effect on the mainline churches in terms of the attention they have received and because they are attracting new members at an astonishing rate.

In addition they have evoked strong criticism from some of the mainline churches because of certain emphases in their theology, particularly their so-called faith teaching which encompasses the prosperity message. Another area in which they are strongly criticised is that of the social gospel. These churches are markedly silent on issues of social justice, which conflicts with, and probably hinders the efforts of the mainline churches in this sphere. The popular media has, over the past few years, paid considerable attention to these new churches, often being equally guilty of the sensationalism of which it accuses them.

As a result of the above-mentioned factors: their rapid growth, their controversial faith teaching, their apparent lack of concern with issues of social justice, their prominence in the media, and hence their effect on social change in South Africa, it was decided that an investigation into these churches in the greater Durban area would be interesting and relevant to the study of ongoing social processes.

CHAPTER 2

HISTORICAL NOTES - PENTECOSTALISM AND THE CHARISMATIC REVIVAL

The term 'pentecost', derived from the Greek word 'pentekoste' (fiftieth), was used to describe the feast of weeks celebrated fifty days after the passover.   According to the New Testament, on this particular day in Jerusalem God poured out his spirit on the disciples who began speaking in other tongues.   The word pentecost is therefore now associated with the baptism of the Holy Spirit with the initial accompanying sign of speaking in other tongues.   (See Cronje, 1980; and Hollenweger, 1972.)

The present-day Pentecostal movement (see Glossary p.197) is generally acknowledged to have had its beginning in a series of revivals that broke out almost simultaneously in many parts of the world (notably in the United States of America) in the early twentieth century.

Although there had been instances of tongues speaking in Christianity prior to 1900, speaking in other tongues suddenly became a central and consistent phenomenon amongst certain groups of Christians.   It was taken as manifest evidence of the baptism of the Holy Spirit. Many small churches grew out of the Pentecostal movement and have since developed into established denominations like Assemblies of God, Full Gospel and various Pentecostal churches.

During the 1960's a charismatic revival developed within mainline Protestant and Catholic churches.   Like the older style Pentecostals, charismatics within the mainline churches were "united by the conviction that they had received the outpouring of God's Holy Spirit".   (Harrell, 1975, p.4.)   Up to the 1960's Pentecostalism had been largely associated with the poor and deprived sectors of society.   When the charismatic revival took hold in the mainline churches, the pentecostal or charismatic experience became an increasingly middle class, hence respectable, phenomenon.

Harrell (1975, p.5) discusses the forces at work in American society

"which allowed the revival to expand from the shabby tabernacles of the poor to the temples of the comfortable". These were:
- the affluence of the time which allowed independent evangelists to build far stronger financial or- ganisations

- the increasing awareness of their own cultural anonymity which made middle class Americans conscious of their own emotional insecurity

- the youth revolt of the '60's which quickly established contact with the fundamentalist religious tradition

- the '60's attraction to occult, psychic phenomena which had close parallels with immediate religious experience and divine healing.

In the 1950's a group of independent revival ministries emerged which Harrell (1975) contends were, to a large degree, responsible for the unexpected growth of Pentecostalism in modern America. Their leaders, who came mostly from classical Pentecostal backgrounds, established independent evangelistic associations/ministries, thus freeing them- selves from the domination of the more established Pentecostal churches. Initially these independent ministries concentrated on healing. Unlike the earlier hell-fire and brimstone preachers "theirs was a signs-gifts-healing, a salvation-deliverance, a Holy Ghost-miracle revival" (Harrell, 1975, p.6). The central theme of the meetings was, according to Harrell (ibid), the miracle.

After 1958 the emphasis in the independent ministries changed. The old healing revival was replaced by a much broader charismatic revival. This was, according to Harrell (1975), due to a number of factors, notably:
1. thousands of people within mainline Christianity had become interested in the charismatic message

2. many thousands were dissatisfied with their own lethargic denominations and were searching for a more dynamic experience.

In response to these factors, most independent evangelists became
teachers more than healers and turned their revival teams into
teaching organisations.   Although healing remained an important
facet of these ministries, they became, according to Harrell (1975),
much more genuinely charismatic, emphasising all the gifts of the
Holy Spirit.   A new feature of these ministries was the emphasis
on prosperity.   "Financial prosperity replaced divine healing
as the most advertised miracle."   (Harrell, 1975, p.8.)

The new churches in South Africa appear mainly to have grown out
of the independent evangelical ministries in the United States of
America.   There is the same emphasis on prosperity and healing
and the same flamboyant style of operation which characterises
evangelical campaigns.   Many of their pastors come from classical
Pentecostal churches as do many of their members.   Neopentecostals
are also swelling membership figures.   The new churches may thus
be seen to be a product of the charismatic revival in general and,
like their independent brethren in America, remarkably adaptive to
the needs of the times.

CHAPTER 3

THE TEACHINGS OF THE NEW CHURCHES

3.1 THE PROSPERITY MESSAGE

It is not clear exactly when and with whom the so-called prosperity message originated. Harrell (1975) says that the belief that God would grant prosperity to his people was an old tenet of the revival movements, even being referred to in the 1930's. It was only in the 1970's that the prosperity message became one of the central tenets of the independent evangelical movement. Some of the most notable proponents of this message are A.A. Allen, Oral Roberts, Kenneth Copeland, Kenneth Hagin Snr. and Jnr., and John Osteen, all of whom head independent evangelical ministries in the United States of America.

It appears that the new churches in South Africa are most closely linked with Kenneth Hagin Ministries Inc. The Rhema churches take their name from Rhema Bible College which is part of Kenneth Hagin's ministry in the United States of America. The head of the Durban Christian Centre acknowledges his indebtedness to Kenneth Hagin and his teachings. Despite the fact that the American ministries are independent from each other and that the new churches in South Africa are not officially connected to each other, the prosperity message appears to be a consistent and unifying feature of all these groups.

Although it is not possible to elucidate fully on this most controversial aspect of the new churches' teachings, a brief summary follows. The Biblical verses most often quoted by pastors, respondents and which appear in the literature are:

> "Give, and it shall be given unto you; good measure, pressed down, and shaken together, and running over, shall men give into your bosom." (Luke 6:38.)

> "What things soever ye desire, when ye pray, believe that ye receive them and ye shall have them." (Mark 11:24.)

> "Beloved, I wish above all things that thou mayest prosper
> and be in health, even as thy soul prospereth."
> (III John :2.)

> "Christ hath redeemed us from the curse of the law.....
> that the blessing of Abraham might come on the Gentiles
> through Jesus Christ; that we might receive the
> promise of the Spirit through faith.   And if ye be
> Christ's, then are ye Abraham's seed, and heirs
> according to the promise."   (Gal. 3:13, 14, 29.)

Basically the prosperity message argues as follows: God wants people
to be prosperous - it is his will for people to prosper (numerous
quotations from the Bible are provided in support of this).   God
made a covenant with Abraham in which many blessings, including
material prosperity, were promised.   Any born-again Christian is
heir to the promises contained in that covenant.   It is the right
of every born-again Christian to expect that God will fulfil his
side of the contract if he/she fulfils certain requirements.

These requirements are:

1. acceptance of Jesus as saviour and Lord

2. operating according to God's laws as opposed to
   natural laws which are beset by inference from
   Satan who comes to steal, kill and to destroy.
   (See John 10:10.)

There are certain laws governing prosperity revealed in God's word.
Faith causes them to function.   An oft quoted phrase is "God's
word works".   These laws of prosperity work the same as the laws
of salvation, healing, etc. and it is the right of every born-again
Christian to work these laws and expect his rights.   "We need to
realise our rights as his children and citizens of the Kingdom of
God."   (Copeland, 1974, p.46.)   Once the conditions of the bargain
have been met, born-again Christians have certain rights - including
divine health, and prosperity - spiritual, financial and otherwise.

Kenneth Hagin in his booklet "How to write your own ticket with God"
(1980a, p.5) describes what Jesus told him in a vision concerning

four principles for getting what the Bible promises:

> "He (i.e. Jesus) said, 'If anybody anywhere, will take these four steps or put these four principles into operation he will always receive <u>whatever he wants</u> from Me or from God the Father'."

The four principles or steps are, according to Hagin:

1. Say it (whatever you say you will get - put words to your faith).

2. Do it (put actions with your faith).

3. Receive it (plug into the power hose of heaven).

4. Tell it (tell others so that they may believe).

They can be used to receive anything in the present tense according to Hagin - "salvation, the baptism of the Holy Spirit, healing for your body, spiritual victory or finances". (Hagin, 1980a, p.6.)

From the outset it is necessary to state that prosperity is not deemed to be financial prosperity only, but all prosperity - there is spiritual prosperity, mental prosperity and physical prosperity.

> "True prosperity is God manifesting Himself to us in His word" (Copeland, 1974, p.23).

> "True prosperity is the ability to use God's power to meet the needs of mankind in any realm of life" (Copeland, 1974, p.26).

Financial prosperity is however certainly not deemed to be bad or ungodly. It is not money that is the root of all evil but the love of money that is the root of all evil. After making the proviso that financial prosperity is not the only kind of prosperity, the tracts on the subject then proceed to use financial and material testimonies almost exclusively to prove the validity of their claims.

According to prosperity teachings, the laws governing financial prosperity are as simple and straightforward as those governing the attainment of any of God's promises: instead of using worldly methods for achieving financial prosperity people must deposit their money with God (by giving in the form of tithes and offerings) who will then give them an inflation-free return on their investments. "Do you want a hundredfold return on your money? Give and let God multiply it back to you. No bank in the world offers this kind of return! Praise the Lord!" (Copeland, 1974, p.67.) "In tithing you are laying the foundation for financial success and abundance. You are establishing deposits with God that can be used when you need them" (Copeland, 1974, p.81).

Tithing is compulsory - a scriptural imperative. One does not give tithes, one brings tithes, as they belong to God anyway. Offerings are given over and above tithes. They are variously called love-offerings, seed giving or miracle offerings, the miracle being that what is invested is returned a hundred-fold. The Holy Spirit often ministers to people telling them where to place their offerings.

The reasons for giving are generally given as follows:
1. In order to help the needy one needs to have something to give.

2. More often the reason for giving is so that one will get back.

> "You do your job and let God do his, thus you will be continually receiving. The more you give the more you will get; the more you get, the more you will have to give..... When you get to this point more will be coming in than you can give away" (Copeland, 1974, p.34).

Although many testimonies refer to receiving money totally unexpectedly after giving, there are also formulas for how to receive from giving. Kenneth Hagin's formula (previously quoted on p.7) can be used, as can Kenneth Copeland's (1974, p.103) which describes specifically how to receive financial blessings.

In order to receive from one's heavenly account, one needs only to confess (which in prosperity teaching means to say something) and then to stand expectantly on God's word (which in this case means having the faith that God will keep his side of the bargain because

one is living according to God's word).   Copeland (1974, p.103)
actually provides 6 steps for obtaining money:

1. Decide on the amount you need: (Be careful not to
   cheat yourself.   God is not a skinflint.)

2. Get in agreement according to Matt. 18:19.

3. Lay hold on it by faith - believe it in your heart and
   confess it with your mouth.

4. Bind the devil and his forces in the name of Jesus -
   order Satan out of your financial affairs.

5. Loose the forces of heaven - when you use the Word in
   the name of Jesus they are obligated to follow your
   command.

6. Praise God for the answer - Father we ask you for $...
   We have this money in our heavenly account and we are
   withdrawing this amount now.   We believe it in our
   hearts and confess now that it is ours.

3.2 SATAN AND SUFFERING

According to the prosperity message, born-again believers are redeemed from the curse of the law, the curse of the law being poverty,
sickness and death (Hagin, 1980b, p.22).   Basically the message is
that poverty and illness are caused by Satan, who oppresses people
in various ways if they are not redeemed from the curse of the law
and are not operating God's laws and meeting the conditions of God's
word.

If not baldly stated, the implications are clear.   Poor people are
poor and sick people are sick because they are not fulfilling certain
spiritual requirements, and are thus subject to the oppression of
the prince of this world, Satan.   Very often in the tracts on the
subject this is not merely implied but stated:

> "The poor consider this a rich man's world.   Satan has
> dominated them with poverty and suppression of all
> kinds.   When you realise that Satan is behind their
> oppression, you will see their need for the power of
> God in their lives" (Copeland, 1974, p.85).

> "We read in Acts 10:38 that God annointed Jesus with the
> Holy Spirit and power - healing power - and He went about
> doing good and healing all who were oppressed of the
> devil. These are the works of God. (This and other
> Scriptures plainly call sickness Satanic oppression.)"
> (Hagin, 1980b, p.19.)

All suffering, whether of a physical, psychological or material nature
is caused, according to the faith or prosperity teachings, by Satan
who either possesses people directly or oppresses people indirectly.
Hagin (1980c, p.6), quoting direct revelation from Jesus says:

> "Every person who is unsaved is dominated and ruled more or
> less by demons and evil spirits, because they are in the
> kingdom of darkness. And many times even folks who are
> saved yield to these spirits and let them dominate them
> more than they should. And if you will let them they
> will because they are there. That's the reason that
> folk do things and don't know why they do them."

There is a distinction in Hagin's writing between demonic oppression
and demonic possession. Oppression is indirect influence by Satan
and his forces, while possession is the literal presence of a demonic
spirit. Illness or psychological problems can be the result of
demonic oppression or possession. When a person is possessed the
demons have to be literally cast out. The decision as to whether
a person is possessed or oppressed by demons is in the hands of the
person (usually the pastor) who has the gift of discerning of spirits.
Hagin (1980c) says that this is not a gift which can be turned on and
off at will - it has to be given by the Spirit.

If demons are directly discerned, they are cast out. Dr. James van
Zyl, a medical doctor and healer associated with the Durban Christian
Centre says: "All sickness is from Satan. Some are more powerful
spirits than others and God usually gives me a word of wisdom in
discerning whether demons have to be cast out or whether healing
will be a creative process..... If a person is demon-possessed
then there is sometimes a manifestation. I just bind them in the
name of Jesus and quote scripture." (Christian New Testament
Times, July 1983, p.9.)

If a person's illness is caused more indirectly through Satanic oppression, Satan is rebuked by the healer.   "It has been our great
joy to see sight restored to blind eyes, hearing returned to deaf
ears, and all manner of sickness healed, as we have boldly exercised
the Christian's right and privilege to rebuke Satan's afflicting
power and command it to leave."   (Fred Roberts in Christian New
Testament Times, July 1983, p.2.)

Psychological problems are also regarded as being directly or indirectly caused by Satan and the same gift of discerning of spirits
is used to assess whether demons have to be cast out.   Hagin (1980c,
p.28,29) quotes a case in which a young man came to him to be healed,
complaining of nervousness and insomnia.   Hagin laid hands on
him and afterwards saw an evil spirit sitting on the man's right
shoulder.   "It had its arm around the man's head and the head was
in an armlock....   I told the evil spirit to leave the man's body,
in the name of Jesus Christ.   When I said that, he turned loose
and fell down on the floor.   When he did that the young man just
hollered out loud and said that it was gone."

To avoid Satanic oppression or possession in their lives, believers
are admonished that the avenue by which Satan enters their lives is
through their minds which are prone to doubt and questioning.   The
way to avoid this is to keep it closed to Satan's influence:
"The only way in the world that the devil can get into the spirit of
a believer is through his mind.   Through his mind."   (Hagin, 1980c,
p.7.) "It does make a difference about what you do with your mind.
You keep it closed to Satan's thoughts and suggestions.   Keep
your mind on Jesus."   (Hagin, 1980c, p.8.)

There is a strong emphasis in faith teachings on health and wealth.
If people are not healed or do not become wealthy, i.e. they are
sick or poor, this is their own faults because they have allowed
Satan into their lives.   The titles of booklets published by
proponents of the faith teachings testify to this thinking:
"Seven hindrances to healing" (Hagin Jnr. 1980), "Don't blame

God" (Hagin, 1980b), "Redeemed from poverty sickness and death"
(Hagin, 1981).

The belief that individuals themselves are responsible and culpable
for their predicaments has profound implications for Christian
responsibility regarding the suffering of others.

3.3 THE SOCIAL GOSPEL AND POLITICAL INVOLVEMENT

Advocates of the so-called social gospel believe that the mission of
the church is "the total task which God has set the Church for the
salvation of the world". (Bosch, 1981, p.47.) This mission, to
be obedient to the Gospel, must therefore involve not only personal
evangelism and salvation, but involvement in the totality of human
existence which necessarily includes the socio-political realm.
Accordingly, the responsibility of the church and of individual
Christians is not only towards themselves and individual
salvation in the hereafter but towards all people in the world in
the present, which includes actively working towards justice and
reconciliation for all people on earth.

Scott (quoted in Bosch, 1981, p.58) describes the above position:

> "An evangelistic invitation oriented toward discipleship
> will include a call to join the living Lord in the work
> of his Kingdom. It will point to specific needs in
> the larger world beyond the individual's private con-
> cerns. It will direct attention to the aspirations of
> ordinary men and women in society, their dreams of
> justice, security, full stomachs, human dignity,
> and opportunities for their children.."

In these terms, involvement in the socio-political realm is an imperative part of Christian duty. This is evidenced by the strong
stand taken by many of the mainline churches on so-called political
issues. Although evangelical churches (see de Gruchy, 1978) are
generally conservative Biblically and politically, shunning any
socio-political involvement, not all evangelicals subscribe to
this position. de Gruchy (1978) and Bosch (1981) both refer to
'radical evangelicalism' which like many of the mainline churches,
encompasses individual salvation as well as active involvement in

rectifying unjust social structures. In South Africa a radical evangelical movement has emerged exemplified by organisations like Africa Enterprise and conferences like SACLA (South African Christian Leadership Assembly). Unlike the traditionally conservative evangelicals who are reluctant to tackle overtly political issues, this new radical branch of the evangelical movement tackles them head on (see Jackson, 1978).

The new churches are not part of this new radical evangelical movement and do not subscribe to or accept the validity of the social gospel, condemning it as being unscriptural.

The new churches are avowedly apolitical, claiming that the mission of the church is purely the saving of souls. The responsibilities of individual Christians are to live a Godly life and to spread the Gospel. Living a Godly life and spreading the Gospel do not include involvement in broader social or political issues.

In support of their lack of involvement with social justice issues the new churches refer to Romans 13:1-2:

> "Every person must submit to the supreme authorities. There is no authority but by act of God, and the existing authorities are instituted by him; consequently anyone who rebels against authority is resisting a divine institution." (The New English Bible.)

The new churches can clearly be categorised as conservative evangelicals in terms of their attitudes towards the social gospel. (For a description of different types of evangelicals see de Gruchy, 1978.)

3.4 FUNDAMENTALISM

Fundamentalism is a belief that the Bible is inspired, inerrant and literally true. The new churches are fundamentalist in their orientation, affirming the absolute authority of the Bible. An interesting addition to their fundamentalism is a common reference in sermons and tracts to direct and divine revelation from God.

When perplexing Biblical questions arise which cannot easily be
answered with an applicable scriptural quotation, reference is made
to Deuteronomy 29:29: "The secret things belong unto the Lord our
God: but those things which are revealed belong unto us and to our
children for ever...."

3.5 CRITICISMS OF THE TEACHINGS OF THE NEW CHURCHES

The prosperity message is the most consistently criticised feature
of the new churches. The late Prof. Trevor Verryn in his booklet
"Rich Christian Poor Christian" gives a succinct theological critique
of the faith/prosperity teachings exemplified by Kenneth Hagin. A
detailed exposition of the criticisms levelled at the teachings of
the new churches by, for example, Verryn (1983) and Magliato (1981)
is not within the scope of this report. However a brief summary
of the most notable criticisms follows:

1. The new churches' claim that health and wealth are
   the perogatives of all Christians is challenged on the
   grounds that there are many references in
   the Bible which emphasise the evils, dangers, self-
   sufficiency, violence and oppression associated
   with money:

   > "But alas for you who are rich, you have
   > had your time of happiness." (Luke 6:24
   > New English Bible.)

   > "Next a word to you who have great possessions.
   > Weep and wail over the miserable fate des-
   > cending on you." (James 5:1-2 New English
   > Bible.)

   > "So wicked men talk, yet still they prosper,
   > and rogues amass great wealth." (Psalm 73:12
   > New English Bible.)

   In addition there are texts calling the disciples to
   poverty and declaring God's blessing of the humble
   poor.

   > "So alas none of you can be a disciple of mine
   > without parting with all his possessions."
   > (Luke 14:33 New English Bible.)

> "We brought nothing into the world, for that
> matter we cannot take anything with us when
> we leave, but if we have food and covering
> we may rest content.   Those who want to
> be rich fall into temptations and snares
> and many foolish harmful desires which
> plunge men into ruin and perdition."
> (1 Tim. 6:7-9.)

Critics claim that the new churches have little to say about texts of the above nature.

2. The notion of 'faith' in the new churches is criticised as being a form of manipulation of God.   The fundamental premise of the faith teachings 'I have observed these rules - therefore God must reward me' is condemned by critics as an attempt at justification by works (akin to the belief of the Sadducees, "upper-class conservatives who put a very high price on success as a sign of divine blessing, and did not baulk at manipulation to attain this end".)(Verryn, 1983, p. 10).

Critics believe that faith in the new churches' teachings becomes faith in faith instead of faith in God.

3. The new churches simplistic explanation of suffering as being purely a sign of being out of God's favour is challenged on a number of points:
   - it does not in any way explain <u>innocent</u> suffering

   - it leads to contempt for the poor and needy and seriously undermines the fundamental Christian virtues of love, charity and compassion

   - it minimises the pain of the cross by denying the reality of the suffering of good Christians in the Bible (cf Job) and in the present.

4. Verryn (1983) claims that the new churches interpret the
   Bible literally only when it suits them. Despite the
   fact that Hagin claims that Mark 11:23-24 ("For verily I
   say unto you, that whosoever shall say unto this mountain,
   Be thou removed, and be thou cast into the sea; and
   shall not doubt in his heart, but shall believe that
   those things which he saith shall come to pass; he
   shall have whatsoever he saith) is the keynote of his
   life and ministry, and despite the fact that he champions
   an extremely literalistic approach to the Bible, and
   nowhere suggests that 'mountain' is a figurative ex-
   pression, there appears to be no example of actual
   mountain moving by Hagin or any of his followers.
   "We are entitled to some explanation for this discrepancy between profession and performance",
   (Verryn, 1983) is a wry comment on the fundamental
   flaw of this literalistic approach to the Bible.

5. The conservative evangelical stance of the new churches
   has been criticised on a number of counts. Sider (1979)
   claims that Jesus and his followers challenged the
   status quo at every point: social, economic, spiritual
   and emotional and that it is the duty of every Christian
   to refrain not only from personal sin but from participation in structural injustice as well. "Cease to do evil
   and learn to do right, pursue justice and champion the
   oppressed," (Isaiah 1:10), is an example of scriptural
   support for the firm conviction that "knowing God is
   inseparable from the costly commitment to the search for
   social justice". (Sider, 1979, p 105.)

   Exclusive concentration on personal salvation-evangelism
   becomes according to critics, pious circular egocentrism.
   "People are brought into the Church with the purpose of
   being sent out to bring others into the church and so on.
   The church thus becomes an end in itself. It collects

and conserves people for heaven; it is a waiting room
for the hereafter."   (Bosch, 1981, p.58.)

6. Additional general criticisms made by Verryn (1983) of the
    theology of the new churches are that they fail to pay
    due attention to:

    Christology   - the nature of Christ as truly God
                            and truly man

    Soteriology   - Christ as saviour

    Ecclesiology   - the nature and role of the church,
                            its authority and ministry

    Sacramentology   - the importance and nature of the
                            sacraments

    Anthropology   - the doctrine of man, his nature
                            and destiny

    Eschatology   - the things of the end - Christ's
                            return, the resurrection of the
                            dead, judgement.

CHAPTER 4

CLASSIFICATION OF THE NEW CHURCHES

It is not possible, within the confines of this study to enter into the complex debate about what constitutes a sect, a church, a cult or a denomination and how the new churches should be classified. A brief exploration of some of these differences will however be made. Depending upon how favourably they are perceived the new churches have been variously called   prosperity cults, manipulationistic sects, the original new testament church or the unified non-denomin-ational church of the end times.

Regardless of how they are classified the new churches possess certain features: they are fundamentalist in terms of their orientation towards the Bible, conservative in terms of their attitude towards social change, charismatic in their emphasis on the Holy Spirit and the gifts of the Holy Spirit and sectarian in terms of their defection from traditional mainline churches.   A brief survey of the literature on church-sect typology and on the distinctive features and growth of Pentecostal, charismatic and conservative churches is thus pertinent and relevant.

4.1 CHURCH-SECT DISTINCTIONS

Weber, and Troeltsch (referred to in Glock and Stark 1973) originally distinguished between churches and sects, showing how sects particularly, functioned to assuage the suffering of the dispossessed.   While churches are an integral part of the social order, stabilising and determining it, sects tend to be hostile or indifferent to secular society. Niebuhr (referred to in Glock and Stark 1973) claimed that sects originate as a haven for the dispossessed but gradually begin to assume church features and become increasingly middle class.

Wilson (1967, p.23) elaborates on the original church-sect distinctions. Typically a sect is identified by the following:

- it is a voluntary association
- membership is by proof to sect authorities of some
    claim to personal merit like knowledge of doctrine
    and affirmation of a conversion experience
- exclusiveness is emphasised
- its self conception is of an elect possessing special
    enlightenment
- personal perfection is the expected standard
- it accepts the priesthood of all believers
- there is a high level of lay participation
- there is opportunity for the member to spontaneously
    express his commitment
- the sect is hostile or indifferent to the secular society
    and to the state
- the commitment of members is always more total and more
    defined than that of members of other religious or-
    ganisations
- the ideology of the sect is much more clearly crystal-
    lised than that of the denomination or church.

Additional characteristics identified by Troeltsch, and Weber (referred
to in Glock and Stark, 1973) are that sects are highly emotional, membership
is of the converted rather than the inherited and they are in tension
with the world.   Niebuhr (ibid) in addition says that sects adopt a
strict and literalistic theology.

In these terms the new churches fit the sect typology very neatly
except for the criterion of hostility or indifference to the state
and secular society.   These churches are at best indifferent and at
worst positively supportive of the state and the current aspirations
of white secular society in South Africa today, for reasons that will
be explained.

4.2 HOW SECTS ARISE

In church-sect theory, sects develop in five distinctive ways according to Wilson (1967):

1. a charismatic figure presents a new teaching and recruits new members

2. they arise as a consequence of internal schism within existing groups

3. they arise spontaneously by the coming together of a group of seekers

4. they arise from attempts to revitalise beliefs and practices within a major religious movement and are associated with attempts to de-institutionalise and de-ritualise church organisation and practice

5. they arise as an unintended consequence of non-denominational revivalism when new converts find assimilation into existing denominations difficult.

It was hypothesised that 1, 4, and 5 above have been contributory factors in the growth of the new churches.

4.3 RECRUITMENT

Evidence from research into the growth of charismatic movements shows overwhelmingly that recruitment is via pre-existing social relationships (family and friends) and not via large-scale public propaganda (Stark and Bainbridge, 1980). Although the decision to be saved or born-again usually takes place in a group setting with all its concomitant pressures, it is considered that attendance at the meeting itself is due to the influence of significant others in the individual's life.

It was hypothesised that recruitment to the new churches would follow the typical pattern and that most people would have joined because of the influence of significant people in their lives.

CHAPTER 5

THEORETICAL APPROACHES

In reviewing the literature on the development and growth of charismatic, fundamentalist and conservative religious movements, eight
broad overlapping theories are relevant.
1. Social disorganisation theories
2. Deprivation theories
3. Theories concerning authoritarianism and political
   conservatism
4. Meaning and belonging theories
5. Personality and life crisis theories
6. Conversion theories
7. Theories of religious experience

5.1 SOCIAL DISORGANISATION THEORIES

Many theorists and researchers have investigated and found a positive
relationship between the degree of economic and social unrest in a
given society and the growth of membership of certain kinds of
religious groups.   (Beckford 1976, Bellah 1978, Sales 1972, O'Dea 1970,
Hine 1974, Photiadis and Schweiker 1970.)

During periods of rapid social change, old norms and values become
irrelevant, inadequate, unsatisfactory and untrustworthy and people
often feel insecure and fearful.   Rapid social change may affect
only a certain sector of society, for example a migrant group who
lose traditional support structures, tend to lose meaningful ties
to the wider society and may experience Durkheimian-type anomie.

O'Dea (1970), investigating the growth of Pentecostal sects amongst
Puerto Rican immigrants in the United States of America refers to
the 'times being out of joint' for people living in a transitional
society.   The resultant anomie gives rise to new and urgent needs.
New religious movements emerge to meet these needs, satisfying the

quest for a sense of community by providing new values to adhere to and new groups to belong to. They thus provide a palliative for the anomie which arises during social disintegration.

During times of rapid and very extensive social disorganisation, it need not only apply to certain sectors of society but can affect all sectors at a given time, for example the social upheaval caused by the great depression of 1930 - 1939. Sales (1972) quotes studies which show that religious conversion rates were much higher during the depression than before or after it. This is attributed to the insecurity and fear engendered by the depression. Sales (1972) found that only certain types of churches become more attractive in times of social disorganisation and stress. These are authoritarian type churches which appeal because of the rhetoric of certainty which they provide. Both Bellah (1978) and Sales (1972) argue that the appeal of fundamentalist evangelical authoritarian churches is that they offer absolute answers to people who have lost the security provided by old norms and values.

5.1.1 Social disorganisation theories and their relevance to the South African situation

In the South African context it is evident that for many whites the times are out of joint. Old norms and values, particularly those pertaining to the invincibility of the white man's position in the present and in the future, have been challenged and shaken. Events such as the township disturbances of June '76, the emergence of militant black trade unionism, the abolition of job reservation, the increasing militance of the black struggle, the liberation of Mocambique and Zimbabwe, the constitutional changes and the economic insecurity created by the recession and the 'abandonment' of the white working class by the National Party, have all contributed to a sense of insecurity and fear about the future.

de Gruchy (1979, p. 188) refers to the fears of white South Africans who are relatively economically secure amidst black poverty. Quoting from the Spro-cas report "Power, privilege and poverty" he suggests reasons for this fear and intransigence. "'The economically secure are suspicious of the aspirations of the insecure, and become repressive and resistant to change, especially where poverty is seen to be related to social and economic impotence. On the other hand, the economically insecure ..... have nothing to lose by militancy and intransigency in their growing demands.' As a result it seems that few white South Africans are without fear for the future."

This fear and insecurity has been exacerbated by the stand of the mainline churches on so-called political issues. The mainline churches have generally become increasingly outspoken and resolute on issues of social justice. No longer can people go to church and be lulled into complacency with sermons that have little or no relevance to the wider society in which they live. The mainline churches have taken stands on mixed marriages, forced removals, apartheid in general, conscientious objection and other controversial social issues. The orientation of many of the mainline churches is towards a future non-racial society with majority rule. Even in the spiritual realm, the security and confidence in old values is being challenged.

The social disorganisation theory appears to explain the growth of the new churches quite successfully. They provide new, albeit illusory certainty with which to face the uncertain future. The faith/prosperity message leaves no room for doubt and insecurity. It is believed that the spirit of God is moving in South Africa and that God is working things out. In this context, all Christians need to do about the situation is to pray.

The hypothesis was then that the appeal of these churches lies partly and largely in the security which they offer in terms of the future of this country. If God has placed the government here, if Christians must submit to those placed in authority over them, if rebellion and chaos are from Satan, then it is clear that these

churches offer a justification to people to remain socially and
politically passive without the niggling guilt and doubt which they
may feel when attending mainline churches and hearing what their
Christian duty ought to be.

The prosperity message, it was hypothesised, suits the economic
insecurity of the times very well. Not only is poverty undesirable
in Christian terms, it is from and of the devil. God wants people
to be prosperous, not only in spiritual and physical terms, but in
financial terms as well.

It was hypothesised that the prosperity message is tailor-made for
relatively affluent white people on two counts. It allays the fears
created by the economic insecurity of the times because once one is
working according to God's laws and his ways one is blessed and cannot
be even financially undermined by the evil one. Secondly it plainly
and simply justifies wealth. One is wealthy, not because one has
been born into a privileged position in society, not because one
exploits workers, not even because one has worked hard and 'earned'
it, but because one is living and working according to God's laws,
and God wants us to be prosperous. Guilt and action regarding the
poverty of others and the vast disparity in the distribution of
wealth in this country is therefore unnecessary and in fact
unscriptural. One's duty towards the poor is simply this: to
convert them to salvational Christianity and to teach them how
to use the 'rules' to work for them. In addition one may help
the needy by being charitable towards them as this in turn brings its own
rewards - financial and otherwise.

In trying to understand how and why the prosperity message appeals to
poorer people it is hypothesised that the many testimonies which
abound in tracts and booklets testifying to more or less instant
prosperity through the use of prosperity principles, gives people a
tangible goal to strive for. "I too can be healthy, wealthy and
prosperous if only my faith is strong enough and I follow the simple
rules."

5.2 DEPRIVATION THEORIES

This category of theories arose from church-sect theory and was based on the study of Pentecostal sects which developed in the first half of this century. The membership of these sects consisted of predominantly working class people, the economically deprived and disinherited classes of society.

Initially economic deprivation was posited as the chief cause of sect development. It was postulated that people who are economically deprived, by becoming sect members, transcend their feelings of deprivation by acquiring feelings of religious privilege which the status of sect member accords them.

The economic deprivation theory could not account satisfactorily for the growth of Pentecostalism and Fundamentalism amongst the middle class. Glock and Stark (1973) thus expanded the concept of deprivation to include "any and all of the ways that an individual may be or feel disadvantaged in comparison to other individuals or groups or to an internalised set of standards". Relative deprivation was now used to explain the attraction to sects, a necessary precondition of this being felt deprivation.

Glock and Stark (1973) distinguish between economic, social, ethical, organismic and psychic deprivation. Social deprivation consists of lack of power, prestige, status and opportunities for social participation afforded the high status members of society. Organismic deprivation is created by physical or mental deformities. Ethical deprivation is created by intense value conflicts where an individual has a firm commitment to a set of values but is unable to live according to these in his particular society (alienation). Psychic deprivation occurs where people are without a meaningful system of values by which to interpret and organise their lives (anomie).

For all these types of deprivation, participation in religious movements, particularly those with strong sect-like characteristics reduces the perceived and/or objective deprivation.

5.2.1 Deprivation theories and their relevance to South Africa

In terms of the budgets of the new churches and in terms of observation of membership composition the traditional socio-economic
deprivation model does not explain the growth of these churches in
South Africa. However in terms of relative ('felt') deprivation,
economic factors may be playing a role. It is suggested that many
people drawn to the new churches, although not members of the
working class, are employed in occupations which are vulnerable and
which foster job insecurity i.e. the sales and distribution sector,
and 'white collar' occupations requiring no formal skills training.
People employed in this sector may perceive themselves to be occupa-
tionally deprived relative to more secure, skilled incumbents, the felt
security deprivation being exacerbated by the burden of long-term
financial liabilities acquired by trying to 'keep up with the Jones's'.

Considering the emphasis in these churches on healing one can
hypothesise that many of the members will be suffering from what
Glock and Stark (1973) call organismic deprivation. Social or
status deprivation theories afford interesting investigation in
the South African context. Gerlach (1974) and Hine (1974) while
investigating whether deprivation played a part in the emergence
and growth of neo-pentecostal churches in the United States of
America found that status or power deprivation was the only type
of deprivation which accounted for the increasing middle class
involvement in these kinds of churches.

McDonnell (1976) points out that one of the chief benefits stated
by adherents to the charismatic movement who have received the
gift of the Holy Spirit is the empowering nature of the experience.
(It is suggested that various factors; social, political and
economic, cause many people to feel that they have no control over
their lives. This feeling of powerlessness is overcome by the
intense experience of being infilled or baptised in the Holy Spirit
which appears to make people feel that they now have the power
which they previously lacked.) It is thus hypothesised that

status deprivation or powerlessness is a factor in accounting for
the success of these churches in South Africa today.

Ethical deprivation is not likely to be a key factor in accounting
for membership of the new churches.   The value systems of members
of the new churches prior to their conversion are not likely to
have been dramatically at variance with the dominant values in
white South African society.   It is more likely that psychic
deprivation will have played a part and that people will,prior to
conversion, not have had a meaningful integrated system of values
to adhere to because old values have been challenged.

5.3 AUTHORITARIANISM

It has already been postulated that authoritarian churches appeal
during times of stress and insecurity because of the certainty
which they provide: absolute answers in a fluctuating, complex and
potentially explosive situation.

Clearly not all people are attracted to authoritarian churches or
organisations even though they may also be experiencing the same
insecurity and disruption.   What factor or factors then lead some
people to join authoritarian organisations or churches while others
join radical political groups or simply remain as they are?

Adorno et al (1950) formulated the idea of a specific authoritarian
personality type typified by the following characteristics:
      authoritarian submission
      authoritarian aggression
      superstition
      overconcern with sexuality
      ethnocentrism
      preoccupation with strength and power.

Threat, in terms of threatening traumatic and overwhelming discipline
in childhood, was seen by Adorno et al (ibid) as being one of the
basic determinants of authoritarianism.

We hypothesised that authoritarian personality types would be
attracted to the new churches because of the authoritarian features
which they (the new churches) display in the following ways:

authoritarian submission	- the new churches insist on submission of wives to husbands, citizens to governments, laity to pastors and pastors to God - also they rely on the absolute authority of the Bible.
authoritarian "aggression"	- although aggression is not the most salient feature, a measure of it is manifest in the disparagement of what is seen as sinful behaviour or people who can be associated with the devil.
superstition	- the mystical and experiential aspects of religion are stressed along with a literal interpretation of the scriptures rather than a more intellectual approach.
ethnocentrism	- the new churches believe that they have the truth and that others are misled or in error: the world is clearly divided into the saved and unsaved.
preoccupation with strength and power	- the new churches repeatedly stress the power which is gained from receiving the Holy Spirit.

Adorno et al (1950) conceived of threat as being a fundamental and
early determinant in the development of the authoritarian personality.
Rokeach (1960, p. 377) reached the same conclusion but felt that threat
in the environment of even mature subjects might influence individuals'
levels of authoritarianism: "The more threatening a situation is to
a person, the more closed (i.e. authoritarian) his belief system will
tend to become."

If our hypothesis is correct: i.e. that the situation in South
Africa today is threatening and generating high levels of anxiety
amongst individuals, then we can postulate that this threat is
increasing authoritarian characteristics in certain authoritarian
people and perhaps stimulating latent tendencies towards authoritarianism
in others and that certain features of the new churches appeal to this
group of people because of their authoritarianism.

Dogmatism (in the sense of a closed belief system), intolerance of
ambiguity, rigidity of thinking and reliance on an external source
of authority (external locus of control) are characteristics which
are strongly correlated with, and often inseparable from authoritarianism.   Consequently it was hypothesised that members of the
new churches would, in addition to being authoritarian, be more
dogmatic, more intolerant of ambiguity and more reliant on an
external source of authority than their mainline counterparts.

Denominational differences have been found on measures of authoritarianism.   Argyle et al (1975), summarising a number of research
findings, state that in general, religious people tend to score
higher than non-religious people; Catholics and fundamentalists
score higher than other religious groups on measures of authoritarianism.   In addition, an inverse relationship has been found
between authoritarianism and humanitarianism.

Stanley (1973a) found that fundamentalist theological students were
more conservative, more certain and more dogmatic than other theological students.   He also found a positive correlation between
dogmatism and a dramatic religious conversion experience as opposed
to a gradual conversion.   Kildahl (referred to in McDonnell, 1976)
is of the opinion that although there is no specific personality
type associated with membership of the charismatic movement,
personality factors do play a major role, specifically the need
to submit to the external guidance of some trusted authority (external locus of control).

5.4 POLITICAL CONSERVATISM

Closely associated with the authoritarian personality is an adherence
to conservative political beliefs. It has generally been found
that people who are authoritarian also hold conservative political
beliefs, which in turn have been found to be differentially associated
with membership of certain kinds of churches.

Using political indices like party preference and voting patterns, a
conservative political ideology has been found to be related to
religious conservatism in the United States of America and Great
Britain (Glock and Stark 1973).   There is considerable debate as
to whether religious conservatism is a cause or a product of
political conservatism or whether they are both merely correlates
of some third factor.

Many theorists in the sociology of religion accept that religious
institutions generally sanction prevailing institutions and hence
the status quo.   Glock and Stark (1973) found that those who cast
their lot with political change are consistently less likely to
participate in church or related activities.   Lipset (in Schneider,
1966) in "Extremism - Political and Religious" hypothesises that
sects drain off the discontent and frustration which would normally
be felt by working class members.   He quotes studies to show that
communists and religious radicals seem to be competing for the
allegiance of the same groups of people.

The mechanisms used by sect/church, and political party for dealing
with the problems of the dispossessed are mutually exclusive.
Sects transvaluate earthly values.   Heavenly rewards are stressed
thus neutralising or undervaluing the importance of earthly material
rewards, and ensuring the passivity of the dispossessed on earth.
(See Thompson, 1968.)   Political parties on the other hand offer
to change things here and now.   Membership of radical political
parties almost necessarily precludes membership of the conservative
fundamentalist/sectarian type churches under discussion.   Although

the membership of the new churches is not predominantly working class it is likely that the new churches perform the same function as sects do in Lipset's terms: i.e. providing an alternative to a political solution for people who do not, it is hypothesised, have any real political 'home' in the South African context.

As has already been discussed, the new churches are conservative theologically and politically. Although they do not sanction prevailing institutions within the church they certainly do sanction the status quo of the society around them. Every meeting contains a prayer for those in authority, and attempts at social change via any method apart from prayer are regarded as being 'in rebellion' which is Satanic.

The Christian Centres in this context serve a double function. Not only do they decry and provide an alternative to political solutions but, unlike their more typical Pentecostal sectarian forbears , they do not transvaluate earthly values. They promise material, earthly well-being in addition to heavenly rewards. They do so by affirming the validity and legitimacy of the prevailing social, economic and political system. Perhaps in this sense they may be seen to be remarkably adaptive and doubly reinforcing of the status quo.

5.4.1 Political conservatism and involvement: relevance to the South African situation

Because of the supposed apolitical stance of the new churches in South Africa it was hypothesised that members would be either in-different to or uninterested in political issues or actively supportive of the ruling Nationalist Party.

In view of the fact that these churches are increasingly becoming a powerful force in South African Christianity it is important to understand whether membership of these churches is actually changing people's political attitudes or whether they are merely attracting people who hold certain kinds of political beliefs.

It was hypothesised that membership of these churches actually changes people's attitudes in the direction of passive if not active support of the status quo because of their Pauline interpretation of submission to authority and the notion that the government is placed here by God.

5.5 MEANING AND BELONGING THEORIES

Social disorganisation, personality and deprivation theories are all based on a premise of abnormality.   The society is in a state of flux, the individual is in some way aberrant or in a situation of crisis, or people are or perceive themselves as being deprived.

Meaning and belonging theories proceed on the assumption that all people have a very real and 'normal' need for two things in their lives: the need for meaning and the need to belong.

In a social situation of stress, where divisions are frequently antagonistic and the problems confronting the society are complex and imminent, the desire of people to find a meaningful and supportive context is enhanced.   South African society characterises this situation.

5.5.1 The need for meaning

Kelly (1977) in 'Why Conservative Churches are Growing' contends that the primary function of any religion is to explain the meaning of life, thus providing adherents with a comprehensive and ultimate world view.   Next its adherents want to feel that they belong to and are part of a supportive communal structure.   Only after these primary needs have been met by the church do people feel that the church should concern itself with broader social concerns.

In support of this hypothesis Kelly asked a broadly representative sample of 3 500 laity to rank order what they considered to be the most important tasks of the local church. The order obtained was as follows:

GROUP A

1. Winning others to Christ

2. Providing worship for members

3. Providing religious instruction

4. Providing ministerial services

5. Providing for the sacraments

GROUP B

6. Helping the needy

7. Supporting overseas missions

8. Serving as social conscience of the community

9. Providing fellowship activities

10. Maintaining facilities for the congregation

11. Supporting the denomination

12. Supporting minority groups

13. Influencing legislation

14. Building low cost housing

Group A Kelley regards as activities which promulgate ultimate meaning. Group B he regards as activities by which meaning is embodied, exercised and practised once it has been acquired. Note that the laity did not reject Group B activities. They regarded them as secondary to Group A activities and objected to the clergy doing B to the exclusion of A.

Although all churches _attempt_ to provide their members with comprehensive and ultimate answers they are not equally successful. Kelley (1977) argues that the quality that enables religious meanings to take hold is not their rationality or logic but rather the _demand_ they make upon their adherents and the degree to which that demand is met by _commitment_. The importance of this insight cannot be over-emphasised.

Kelley argues that growth occurs not in spite of demand but because
of it.   In the United States of America, conservative churches like
Assemblies of God and Holiness churches, are growing at a rapid rate
while other more liberal ecumenical churches are losing members.
The social strength of conservative churches derives from the fact
that they make high demands and require total commitment from their
members.   His main hypothesis is that social strength and leniency
(i.e. in the form of tolerance, liberalism and ecumenicity) do not
go together.   A religious group with evidences of social strength
will proportionately show traits of strictness.   It is precisely
this strictness which establishes and reinforces meaning for members.   Strictness is a consequence of and evidence of the serious-
ness of meaning of the religious group.

Kelley identifies various indicators of social strength which have
corresponding traits of strictness deriving from them.   These can
be seen below:

A.   INDICATORS OF SOCIAL STRENGTH   B.   TRAITS OF STRICTNESS
    1. Commitment   Absolutism

    2. Discipline   Conformity

    3. Missionary zeal   Fanaticism

Commitment   -   willingness to suffer and sacrifice
                                 for the cause; a total response to
                                 a total demand

Absolutism   -   an uncritical attachment to a single
                                 set of values; the conviction that
                                 the group has the monopoly on truth;
                                 a closed system explaining everything

Discipline   -   willingness to obey commands without
                                 question

Conformity   -   intolerance of internal dissent;
                                 conformity facilitated by perse-
                                 cution or ridicule by outsiders

| Missionary zeal | - | the desire to spread "the good news" and convert others to the same cause |
| Fanaticism | - | a one-way flow of communication with outsiders; an unwillingness or inability to conduct dialogue with conflicting viewpoints. |

As evidence for his hypothesis, Kelley shows that the churches which are growing in the United States of America (Assemblies of God, Pentecostal, Holiness and Evangelicals), are all strict and socially strong. This he argues, is not despite, but because of the fact that they are unreasonable, unsociable (in the sense of being uninterested in social concerns), other-worldly, intolerant and non-ecumenical.

Churches which are less strict; more liberal, ecumenical, prepared to tolerate diversity, which foster dialogue, and which engage in social concerns, are lacking in social strength and are consequently declining.   Conservative churches are more successful because they are giving certain people what they want.   What such people want is for the meaning of life to be made simple for them.

5.5.2 Belonging

The provision of a sense of belonging by the church, as far as Kelley is concerned, is integral but secondary to the provision of meaning. A sense of community (belonging) is vital in the formation and main-tenance of religious beliefs and hence meaning, but the provision of meaning is the ultimate priority of the church.

McGaw (1979, 1980) accords a far more central position to the provision of belonging. He compared two different kinds of congregations (a neo-Pentecostal and a traditional mainline congregation) in terms of how well they satisfied their members' needs for meaning and

belonging.   Religious commitment was viewed in terms of meaning and
belonging.   Meaning was defined as the cognitive and ideological
dimension of religion while belonging was defined as the communal
structure and ability of the religious group to integrate beliefs
and practices.

McGraw measured meaning in terms of the following:
- orthodoxy and unanimity of beliefs

- particularism (salvation limited to Christians)

- public worship

- fellowship and giving

- education and growth

- social gospel

Belonging was measured in terms of the following:
- ritualism

- donations

- hours per week in church activities

- number of closest friends belonging to same church.

On all measures of meaning and belonging the neo-Pentecostal group was
more religiously committed than the traditional group.   McGaw (1979,
1980) claims that the nature of beliefs seems no more important than
the social context in which they are presented.   Beliefs provide the
motivation and legitimation for group activities while the activities
provide the social context in which beliefs are formed and reinforced.

5.5.3   Involvement with social concerns

According to Kelley's (1977) findings, the laity feel that the church
should concentrate on activities which promulgate ultimate meaning
(Group A).   These activities do not include wider social concerns.
Kelley's hypothesis concerning social strength and strictness would
seem to imply that for a church to be socially strong it must be

conservative, and not primarily concern itself with issues of social justice.   It would also seem to imply that those churches which focus on wider social issues as a priority are not going to be successful or grow.

Kelley does acknowledge that it is not involvement with social issues per se that has caused the relative demise of the mainline churches.   The decline is because of the fact that the mainline churches have undertaken social action in ways that do not make clear how the social action fits in with and is required by the meaning system of the church.

If this is not made clear and an absolutely integral part of the belief system, churches will merely end up telling members what they ought to be doing in the social context in the hope that they will somehow recognise and do their duty.   He believes that there is insufficient commitment or discipline in the mainline churches to overcome the worldly interests of members.   Thus they judge the church's directives in terms of their own secular interests which may often conflict with social intervention or change.

5.6 MEANING AND BELONGING: APPLIED TO THE SOUTH AFRICAN CONTEXT

Clearly the provision of meaning in the South African context is pertinent to the social disorganisation theory.   Particularly in times of stress and insecurity people need an explicitly coherent explanation for understanding:

- their position in society

- why suffering exists on an individual and societal level

- what their responsibilities are in relation to that suffering

- what is happening around them

- what is going to happen to them.

As has already been discussed, the new churches appear to provide
a simple and comprehensive system of meaning to explain to members
what is happening to and around them in South Africa today.

5.6.1 Ranking of church tasks

The hypothesis, with reference to the respondents in the present
sample, was that the priorities of all groups would be similar to
those of Kelley's sample but that the new church group particularly
would not only rate Group B type activities as being of secondary
importance for the church, but would reject 'political activities'
completely.   New church members in an already rapidly changing
society which may be threatening to them, would tend to shy away
from political activities that may hasten such change.

5.6.2 Evidences of social strength and traits of strictness

It would seem that the new churches are, in Kelley's terms, socially
stronger and more strict than their mainline church counterparts.
The following areas required investigation:

Commitment:

It was hypothesised that the greater commitment of new church members
would be evident in a dramatic change in personal and social life.

Absolutism:

Bearing in mind that there is a close link between absolutism and
authoritarianism we hypothesised that the new churches and members
would believe that they had the truth and that others were in error,
that they would have a closed system of meaning and value explaining
everything and that they would have an uncritical and unreflective
attachment to a single set of values.   It was hypothesised that
absolutism was facilitated by literal fundamentalist beliefs, that
all charismatics would have fundamentalist beliefs and that there
would be greater unanimity of belief amongst the new church charismatic respondents than amongst other groups.

Discipline:

This characteristic is also associated with authoritarianism. We
hypothesised that the new church charismatics would be willing to
accept the authority of their leadership without question and the
authority of the Bible without question.   In addition, it was
hypothesised that new church charismatics would subscribe to the
belief that wives should submit to the authority of their husbands.

Conformity:

We hypothesised that the new church charismatics would be intolerant
of dissent and that there would be many shared stigmata of belonging -
signs or cues which immediately distinguish members from non-members
e.g. language usage, and other non-verbal symbols.

Missionary zeal:

We hypothesised that the new church charismatic group would be eager
to convert others to their way of thinking, and that internal
communications would be stylised and highly symbolic.

Fanaticism:

It was hypothesised that the new church charismatics would be fanatical
in the sense of allowing only certain selected information into their
consciousness and that their value system would exemplify intolerance
of different and conflicting world-views.

5.6.3 Measures of belonging

Ritualism:

It was hypothesised that the new church charismatic group would attend
church more often than other groups.

Donations:

It was hypothesised that the new church charismatic group would donate
relatively more money to the church than other groups as an indication
of their commitment and as a consequence of the prosperity message.

Time spent in church activities:

It was hypothesised that new church charismatics would spend more
hours per week in church activities than other groups and that the
nature of these activities would be in the area of individual immediate Group A type activities rather than in the area of social
justice community-orientated activities.

Number of closest friends belonging to same church:

Following on from a complete change in social life it was hypothesised
that the new church charismatic group would have more close friends
belonging to the same church than other groups.

5.7 PERSONALITY THEORIES AND LIFE CRISES

These theories are based on the assumption that individuals who are
maladjusted or emotionally unstable are attracted to the emotional
Pentecostal/Charismatic movements.   Conversion to these movements
has been related to various abnormal psychological processes:
neuroticism, repressed hostility towards the father, high manifest
anxiety, fear of death, guilt, high hypnotic suggestibility and
inability to deal with conflicts   (Gibbons et al 1972, Spellman et
al 1971, Salzman 1953, Ness et al 1980, Argyle et al 1975.)

It is suggested by theorists and researchers in this area that the
above psychological factors indicate a 'conversion type' personality,
predisposing the individual exhibiting these characteristics, to
having a dramatic salvational experience.   Serious life crises,
for example, death of a loved one, fear of own death, serious illness, marital and family problems, financial crises, and employment
problems are likely to precipitate a conversion experience.

A fundamentalist personality type has been identified as having: a
marked degree of covert hostility, a pervasive masochism, frequent
use of paranoid mechanisms, frequent psychosomatic symptoms, a
depressive tenor, conflicts over sexual identity and excessive
dependence (Stanley, in Brown 1973).   Authoritarianism (already

discussed) may also be regarded as a personality characteristic.

Although it is extremely difficult to establish the existence of
personality traits like hysteria, neuroticism and hypnotic suggestibility, particularly within the confines of a survey of this
nature, certain trends were expected.

On the basis of the generalisation that converts to Pentecostal/
Charismatic movements are likely to have had either personality
problems or experienced serious life crises prior to conversion
the following hypotheses were formulated: members of the new
churches would have, in their pre-conversion state, been
- more guilty

- more anxious

- more depressed

- more fearful

- more insecure
than their mainline counterparts.

It was also hypothesised that members of the new churches would have
been more likely to have experienced serious life crises prior to
their conversion than members of the mainline churches and that this
would have been a contributory factor in their conversion to the new
churches.

5.8 CONVERSION THEORIES

Glock and Stark (1973, p.6) define conversion as "the process by which
a person comes to adopt an all-pervading world view or changes from
one such perspective to another".   It is characterised by a major
discontinuity in behaviour and a wrenching of the personality.   The
convert apparently experiences a drastic shift in the orientation of
his valuation of reality.

Some authors like Salzman (1953) believe that conversion can be a

gradual or a dramatic process. The 'born-again' experience is
however a decisive one which can be located in time and place. A
salvational experience is explicitly required by charismatic
churches. Glock and Stark (1973, p.48) contend that these church
bodies have developed "well-organised and institutionalised
mechanisms to generate and channel predispositions for salvational
experiences".

Typically according to Glock and Stark (1973) the salvational
experience is the consequence of a build-up of group pressure,
notably the building up of a sense of sin and guilt which is
triggered by the pleading and urging of preacher, congregation,
and often close friends (during meetings specifically intended
for saving souls). Although a salvational experience can occur
individually it is more likely to occur in a group situation
evidenced by the high percentage of converts at evangelical campaigns.

The conversion experience apparently precipitates a drastic change
in the individual's life. Although it is acknowledged that there
are usually multi-faceted pre-conversion factors accounting for
this dramatic change, there are certain factors which together
facilitate a conversion experience, and foster changed attitudes.

Argyle et al (1975) elaborate on these factors accounting for
attitude change in the light of the evangelical campaigns of Billy
Graham.

   Emotional appeals: people are far more suggestible when
                 they are in a state of emotional ex-
                 haustion and arousal. This is in-
                 duced by various techniques like
                 repetition, rhythmic dancing and
                 drumming, deliberate concentration
                 on intended converts, music and
                 highly emotional hymns sung by many
                 people.

Anxiety arousal:	up to a point anxiety arousal produces greater attitude or behaviour change than when anxiety is not aroused. This is induced in religious meetings by constant repetition and other oratorical devices, particularly those emphasising that tomorrow may be too late.
Public commitment:	public commitment has an effect on attitudes. This increases the likelihood of the person maintaining the commitment. Evangelical campaigns and charismatic churches have a salvation or altar call in which people are required to go forward and make a public commitment.
Personal influence:	this plays an important part in attitude change. In evangelical campaigns there is initially the influence of the speaker, followed by the influence of counsellors who individually counsel the new recruits immediately after the experience of salvation.
Characteristics of speaker:	a well-respected, vaunted, charismatic speaker is more likely to induce attitude change.

It was hypothesised that for all charismatics in the sample the conversion experience would have been dramatic and emotional and that it would most often occur in a group setting.

It was also hypothesised that the form and style of the services at the new churches would foster attitude change in the following ways:

emotional appeals

anxiety arousal

public commitment

personal influence

characteristics of speaker.

5.9 RELIGIOUS EXPERIENCE

The experience of being saved in Christ or born-again is usually
accompanied by intense physical and emotional sensations.   Conway
and Siegelman (1981, p.40) elaborate on the intense physical sensations which accompany the "born-again" moment: "A tingling of
energy appears to be common, along with alternating feelings of
heat and cold.   Frequently, the individual will have the impression
of a cleansing flow of water, which is usually accompanied by an
uncontrollable surge of tears."

Apart from the conversion experience itself which is the initial
act of commitment, there are other varieties of religious experience
which reinforce the original commitment and which assure the members
of the group that their belief system is correct.   Some authors
refer to these experiences as bridge-burning acts because they
signify and reinforce acceptance of the new belief system (McDonnell
1976).   Depending on one's theoretical perspective these varieties
of religious experience can be referred to as altered states of
consciousness, religious mysticism, religious hysteria or a sign
of visitation by the Divine.

Within the charismatic movement in general there are certain religious
experiences which are regarded as compulsory.   The first is the experience of "being saved".   The second is the baptism or infilling
of the Holy Spirit which is evidenced by speaking in tongues
(glossolalia).   There is considerable controversy about the
phenomenon of glossolalia both theologically and sociologically.
Without entering into the debate the following broad issues should

be mentioned: within charismatic Christianity there is debate
as to whether glossolalia is the sign of being infilled with the
Holy Spirit or whether it is only one of the signs, edifying,
empowering and enriching but not essential (i.e. a sufficient
though not a necessary condition). There appears to be general
agreement amongst charismatics that speaking in tongues has beneficial effects.

Within psychological and sociological research into glossolalia
there is also considerable dispute. Some researchers have pointed
to the cathartic effects to the individual of speaking in tongues.
Others suggest that it is only neurotic, hypnotically suggestible
people who speak in tongues. Early deprivation theories regarded
glossolalia as a disreputable phenomenon occurring only amongst the
economically deprived sectors of society. As the charismatic
movement became an increasingly middle class phenomenon, glossolalia
came to be regarded as reputable and normal.

Other gifts of the Holy Spirit are highly regarded amongst charismatics
and are often accompanied by intense physical sensations. We hypothesised that religious experiences would be valued by all charismatics
in the sample, and that these experiences would be vital in confirming
beliefs.

CHAPTER 6

METHODS EMPLOYED IN THE STUDY

BACKGROUND INTERVIEWS

This largely exploratory investigation was conducted in the greater Durban area. Pastors of the new churches were informally interviewed and asked questions about their theology, reasons for their growth, their membership and their attitudes to various issues in the wider secular society. Ministers of various mainline churches and theologians were interviewed and asked about their attitudes towards the new churches.

New church services were attended by the interviewers in an attempt to gain additional insight into the new church phenomenon. On the basis of interviews with pastors, ministers and members of the new churches, with the various hypotheses in mind, an interview schedule for a lay sample (see Appendix 3) was drawn up after a small pilot study.

Section A of the questionnaire consisted of original items, apart from item 13 which was taken from a survey by Assumption Catholic Parish, Durban. Sections B and C consisted of individual items taken from a variety of sources (see Appendix 4). The questionnaire therefore makes no pretence at being a standardised test or a scale but provides indices of attitudinal and behavioural tendencies among groups in the sample.

THE SMALL SAMPLE SURVEY

Given the nature of the topic of this research, the sampling could not be rigorous. No sampling frame of members of the new churches exists. Therefore the key focus group had to be sampled by means of a rough quota sample based on broad estimates of the social profiles of the new church group.

Given this enforced method, the most appropriate way of sampling
the other religious categories was by employing the same approach,
attempting to "match" the samples by obtaining similar age and
sex profiles. Samples could not be "matched" on other characteristics because these differ substantially between the religious
groups.

Funding constraints limited the size of the sample to 80 lay members of
various churches. It was decided under these circumstances to limit
the sample to white people because the membership of the new churches
is predominantly white, and because comparisons between people of
different races would, in the South African context of racial segregation, have introduced variables which would have enormously com-
plicated the enquiry, the effect of which would have been to raise
issues which were not germane to the study. The survey is consequently exploratory rather than rigorous.

Thirty members of the Durban Christian Centre were interviewed. The
Durban Christian Centre was chosen because it is by far the largest
new church in the greater Durban area and is centrally situated. In
addition, 50 members of established churches were interviewed.
The established church sample was drawn from 5 different denominations:
Roman Catholic, Anglican, Methodist, Presbyterian and Full Gospel
(see Table 51, p.192). The particular congregations representing
each denomination were chosen because of their geographical proximity
to each other and because that area of Durban was considered to be
more-or-less equivalent in terms of socio-economic status to the area
from which the new church sample was drawn.

Ministers of the five congregations mentioned were approached and
asked to provide names of members of their congregations. They
were asked to present as broad a range as possible in terms of
religious commitment, age, sex and occupation. The names of the
thirty Christian Centre members were obtained from pastors and from
home fellowship group leaders in the same geographical area as the
five established congregations.

Of the fifty established church members chosen, twenty
considered themselves to be born-again Christians. They provided
useful comparisons with the new church charismatic sample because
they were part of the charismatic movement in general, being theo-
retically different from the new church charismatic sample only in
their allegiance to their particular established denominations.

The survey results were thus analysed in terms of the following
groupings:

New church charismatics (N.C.C.) - 30

Established church charismatics (E.C.C.) - 20

Mainline church traditionalists (i.e. non-charismatics)
(M.C.T.) - 30

Of the total sample half the respondents were male and half female
(see Table 54, p.193). The 3 sample groups were also equally divided
into males and females. An attempt was made to interview as broad
an age range as possible within the 3 sample groups (see Table 55 p.194).
Approximately half of each sample group (50% of the new church
charismatic respondents, 55% of the established church charismatic
respondents, and 50% of the mainline church traditional respondents)
were under 40 years of age. The majority of the total sample were
married (60% of new church charismatics, 70% of established church
charismatics and 73% of mainline church traditionalists - see Table
56, p.194).

As far as formal educational level was concerned, (see Table 57, p.195),
approximately half the total sample (67% of new church charismatics,
55% of established church charismatics and 50% of mainline church
traditionalists) had passed Std. 10 or below, with significantly
fewer mainline church traditionalists than charismatics having an
educational level below Std. 10. New church charismatics were
significantly underrepresented in the degree category (3%) as
compared with 35 percent of established church charismatics and
27 percent of mainline church traditionalists.

As regards occupation, (see Table 58, p. 195) there were fewer
housewives in the mainline church traditional sample, more
professional and managerial occupations in the established church
sample and more people operating for individual profit or commission
in the new church charismatic sample. The mean income (see Table 59,
p. 195) was R1 150, for the new church charismatic sample, R823
for the established church charismatic sample and R1 100 for the
mainline church traditional sample.

The respondents were all telephoned and their co-operation established prior to the interviews. Interviews took an average of
three hours with the new church charismatic respondents and an
average of one-and-a-half hours with the rest of the sample. The
difference in time taken for interviews, despite the use of the
same interview schedule, was due to the fact that the new church
charismatic respondents were more voluble and eager to relate their
experiences and opinions than the rest of the sample. Most of the
interviews took place in the respondents' homes with the remainder
taking place at respondents' places of work.

To establish the actual and potential scope of the membership of
new churches, a question concerning religious affiliation was
included in a Market Research Africa Omnijet Survey (see Appendix
5, p.222). This survey was conducted in September 1983 using a
random sample of 500 white adults in cities, towns and villages in
Natal.

We are fully aware that this study is not as rigorous in statistical
and sampling terms as we would have liked it to be. However, it
represents an exploratory piece of research and as such was intended
to provide insights into trends and tendencies rather than measurable
differences between religious categories. Furthermore, the nature of
the interviewing was such as to require great persuasion and tact,
and we felt it more appropriate to concentrate on valid and sensitive
interviews than on statistical precision.

As regards comparisons between church groups we are aware that
sampling error could lead to false patterns simply because of an
over - or under-representation of people in a particular age or
occupational category. However, our findings show consistently
that, as regards major aspects of attitudes and behaviour, differences
in religious allegiance overshadow differences in terms of sex,
age, occupation or level of education. It is highly unlikely that
sample bias could affect our cautious conclusions.

We have not generalised on the basis of single items or isolated
findings*. Trends have been identified only where several aspects of
the data point in the same direction. Therefore, as a qualitative
rather than a quantitative exercise, we consider the results to be
broadly valid and sufficiently reliable for the purpose of the
investigation.

CHAPTER 7

FACTUAL INFORMATION ABOUT NEW CHURCHES IN THE GREATER DURBAN AREA

7.1 HOW THE NEW CHURCHES HAVE ARISEN

Pastors of the new churches were asked how their churches had started
and why they had broken away from the established traditional churches.
The replies were unanimous in that all of them said that they had been
led by God or the Holy Spirit after a great deal of often painful
'soul-searching', meditation, fasting and prophecy. The consensus
in summary was that there was a great, unprecedented Christian revival
in South Africa, that the Holy Spirit was moving and that one either
had to move with the Holy Spirit or get left behind.

Channel magazine, which appears to be the mouthpiece of the new churches
in South Africa, claims that during 1982 there were 6 major establishments
that were "mainly instrumental in propagating the word of God and allowing
the Spirit to move according to the will of God" (Channel. Jan./Feb. 1983, p.4).
The six churches which are identified as having done more towards establishing the gospel on earth than most other establishments put
together in the history of Christianity in South Africa are:

Christ for all Nations

Rhema

Bedfordview Christian Centre

Hatfield Baptist Church

Nicky van der Westhuizen's tent tabernacle

Fred Roberts' Christian Centres (Durban and East Rand)

It is claimed that "the hunger for reality and the need for truth are
the driving forces of this revival" (Channel Jan./Feb. 1983, p.21).

In an article in Channel magazine, Fred Roberts, the head of Durban
Christian Centre, writes that God spoke to him and said:

> "I'm going to send a revival to South Africa such as you
> have never witnessed before or the nation has never wit-
> nessed before.   It's going to be a revival that will
> sweep from the Southern tip of the Cape and will sweep
> right up into Africa." (Channel Jan./Feb. 1983, p.19.)

The established churches from which they had come were, according to
the pastors, restricting the move of the Holy Spirit by not allowing
them (the pastors) to move freely where they were being led.   This
restriction they felt was due to the bureaucracy and hierarchical
authority structure of the established churches who had become so
involved with form and tradition and 'man-made rules' that they were
blinded to what was happening around them.   The pastors had thus
been forced to move out of the denominational churches altogether
and establish their own non-denominational churches which were now
free to move according to God's timing rather than man's, and were
subject only to the authority of God.   The pastors interviewed
were unanimous that their churches were the vanguard of the move
towards the unified non-denominational church signifying the 'end
times'.

The following quotes by Fred Roberts typify the rationale and language
style used by new church pastors:

> "Now another wave is coming and it's the final wave
> of the Spirit before Jesus comes..... By the year
> 2000, if Jesus tarries that long, there won't be
> many people in the church any longer - most of them
> will have left.....   There are hundreds of people
> looking for spiritual homes right now....
>
> We want to belong to something that hasn't got a tag
> to it.   The names of denominations are growing dimmer
> and dimmer while the name of Jesus gets brighter and
> brighter."   (Channel Jan./Feb. 1983, p.20.)

The new churches in the greater Durban area, all of whom are independent
of each other, started in the following ways:

Durban Christian Centre   - Fred Roberts, a Full Gospel Minister,
(3 000 people)   left the Full Gospel church taking
                                     some of the congregation with him.
                                     The Durban Christian Centre was
                                     started with 100 people in 1979. It
                                     now has a number of outreaches (see
                                     Table 1, p.57).

Pinetown Christian Centre (700 people)	- Rod Seago, a Full Gospel minister with Fred Roberts, left the Full Gospel church taking some of the congregation with him. The Centre started in 1982 in Pinetown with 100 people.
Bible Fellowship (previously Highway Christian Centre) (250 people)	- Neville de Witt, an elder of the Presbyterian church, left to establish a new church in Pinetown taking approximately 10 of the congregation with him. The Centre started in 1981 with 15 people.
Victory Faith Centre (400 people)	- Rob Rufus, an Invisible Church pastor established a church in Pinetown under the auspices of the Invisible Church. Once it had been established it was decided to break away from the Invisible Church and become independent. The Invisible Church started in 1979 with 25 people, becoming independent early in 1982.
Living Word Centre (200 people)	- Errol Arde, a Durban Christian Centre Bible College graduate (ex Roman Catholic) established a centre in Westville which started in 1982 with 5 people.

Rhema Bible Church (300 people)	- John Ireland, a graduate of Rhema Bible College Johannesburg (ex Methodist) established his church in Durban North in 1980 starting with 35-40 people.
Westville Christian Fellowship (90 people)	- Dave Philips, a lay preacher in the Anglican church, established his church in Westville in 1983 beginning with a group of people from his Anglican Bible Study group. The church started with 20 people.

(Note that during the course of this study, other churches have started with small groups of people. 'Established' new churches in Amanzimtoti and Ballitoville have been excluded in view of their being outside of the greater Durban area.)

7.2 ORGANISATION

Of all the new churches identified, Rhema Bible Church was the only one having structural links with other churches, namely other Rhema Bible Churches with headquarters in Johannesburg. The Durban Christian Centre has outreaches in Wentworth, Chatsworth, Queensburgh, Clare Estates, Newlands East, Umlazi, KwaMashu and Mariannridge. These centres are thus part of the Durban Christian Centre, which is the largest new church in Durban. There are no structural links between the Durban Christian Centre and the other churches identified in Table 1 (p.57).

All the new churches identified claimed to be completely independent, having no organisational links with any other churches. Each has its own constitution and is registered as a company established not for gain, thus being exempt from taxation.

Although there are no structural links between the various new churches in Durban the pastors say that they 'fellowship' together, share the

same beliefs and ideals, and cooperate in the sharing of overseas
speakers and marriage officers.   Some of the new church pastors are
marriage officers.   It appears that this has been achieved in Durban
chiefly by the formation of Christian Fellowship International (CFI)
which is registered by the government as a denomination and therefore
has recognised marriage officers.

Christian Fellowship International is defined by the new church pastors
as a covering body of pastors.   Its chief aim is for pastors to get
together on a monthly basis for 'fellowship and encouragement'.   Fred
Roberts of the Durban Christian Centre is its chairman, and anyone who
identifies with the aims and objectives of Christian Fellowship International and is part of it, comes under its authority.   This does not,
in the opinion of pastors who are members of Christian Fellowship
International, in any way jeopardise the autonomy and independence of
their own churches and in no way resembles the hierarchical structure
of established denominations.

Individual pastors register with Christian Fellowship International,
described by a member of the Durban Christian Centre staff as *"a
fellowship of the sent ones"*.   Pastors from Pinetown Christian
Centre, Living Word Centre, and various Christian Centres in Natal
are members of Christian Fellowship International.

7.3 MEMBERSHIP

It was difficult to establish precise membership figures for the
new churches in Durban and surroundings as pastors were generally
resistant to the term 'member' because of its denominational connota-
tions.   Total membership figures quoted in Table 1 below are therefore largely based on attendance at services.   Where people formally
become members or partners of the particular church this figure is
indicated in brackets.

Some record of membership is kept by the new churches with different
churches employing different recording methods.   For example the
Durban Christian Centre asks visitors to fill in visitors cards;
when people go forward to be saved in the services their personal

details are recorded by counsellors for follow-up purposes; in order to be truly identified with the Durban Christian Centre (DCC), people must attend 'Spiritual Growth Seminars' (10 lessons about the DCC's doctrine) at the Bible College for a week, after which they are baptised in water and then 'welcomed into the family'. They are then considered to be fully committed to the Durban Christian Centre.

Other new churches make more formal demands on their members. Bible Fellowship in Pinetown for example requires that full members tithe and are born-again, 'spirit-filled', water-baptised believers. Although tithing is taught and expected in all the new churches it is not generally compulsory for membership.

New church pastors were asked under what conditions they might ask a member to withdraw. The most consistent reason given was if a member caused strife or division in the church, or if a member persisted in behaving in an unChristian manner e.g. adultery or homosexuality.

7.4 <u>MEMBERSHIP FIGURES AND COMPOSITION</u> (see Table 1, p. 57).

The new churches identified have a predominantly white membership (80%), followed by an Indian membership of 10%, a coloured membership of 8% and an African membership of a mere 2%. From Table 1, p. 57 it can be seen that a comparatively high percentage of members (32%) attend Home Fellowship (Bible Study) groups. This is consistent with the small cell strategy of the new churches ('dividing in order to multiply'). In addition to Home Fellowship groups most new churches have Women's Fellowship groups, Youth groups and Children's Church. Most new church pastors interviewed noted that their youth groups were particularly popular because young people especially enjoyed the modern approach which they offered and were consequently 'on fire for the Lord'.

** TABLE 1: FACTUAL DETAILS ABOUT NEW CHURCHES IN THE GREATER DURBAN AREA

	TOTAL* "MEMBER- SHIP"	% WHITE	% INDIAN	% COLOURED	% AFRICAN	% IN HOME FELLOW- SHIP	% IN WOMEN'S GROUP	% IN YOUTH GROUP	% IN YOUNG ADULTS GROUP	% IN CHILDREN'S CHURCH	SERVICES	ATTEN- DANCE	VENUE	SALARIED STAFF
Durban Christian Centre	3 000 (inclu- des out- reaches below)	70	15	13	2	33	20	10	0	13	Sun. am / pm	1 800 / 1 200	Embassy	15 (9 pastors 6 admin.)
- Wentworth	(250)	(6)	(2)	(91)	(1)	(0)	(20)	(26)	(7)	(0)	Thurs. pm / Sun. pm	250 / 250	Community Centre	-
- Chatsworth	(150)	(2)	(95)	(2)	(1)	(53)	(33)	(0)	(0)	(23)	Sun. am / Wed. pm	150 / 150	Tent	-
- Clare Estate	(40)	(0)	(100)	(0)	(0)	(0)	(0)	(0)	(0)	(0)	-	40	-	-
- Newlands East	(40)	(0)	(0)	(100)	(0)	(0)	(0)	(0)	(0)	(0)	-	40	-	-
- Mariannridge	(25)	(0)	(0)	(100)	(0)	(0)	(0)	(0)	(0)	(0)	-	25	-	-
- Umlazi	(60)	(0)	(0)	(0)	(100)	(0)	(0)	(0)	(0)	(0)	-	60	-	-
- KwaMashu	(80)	(0)	(0)	(0)	(100)	(0)	(0)	(0)	(0)	(0)	-	80	-	-
- Queensburgh	(130)	(100)	(0)	(0)	(0)	(77)	(35)	(0)	(0)	(0)	Sun. pm	80	Hall	-
Pinetown Christian Centre	700	93	5	1	1	30	15	10	6	15	Sun. am / pm	450 / 275	School	10 (4 pastors 2 admin. 2 ministries)
Victory Faith Centre	400	95	3	1	1	37	-	8	-	13	Sun. am / pm	200 / 350	Rented Premises	4 (2 pastors 1 admin. 1 ministry)
Bible Fellowship	250 (150 members)	97	2	-	1	20	18	12	-	24	Sun. am / pm	80 / 60	School	4 (2 pastors 2 admin.)
Rhema Bible Church	300 (180 partner- ships)	91	3	5	1	53	20	7	12	23	Sun. am / pm	400 / 300	Metro	5 (2 pastors 2 admin. 1 ministry)
Living Word Centre	200	100	-	-	-	10	35	15	-	30	Sun. am / pm	120 / 75	School	? (1 pastor 1 admin.)
Westville Christian Fellowship	90	100	-	-	-	25	10	28	-	22	Sun. pm	90	Hall	No full time
TOTALS	4 940	80	10	8	2	32	18	10	2	15				

* Total "membership" - this generally indicates attendance at services and includes children and youth. Where people have specifically become formal members this is indicated in brackets.

** All figures are approximations according to pastors' estimates in June 1983 - no formal records were examined.

- Information not obtained.

Approximately 5000 people appear to be members of new churches in the greater Durban area. When compared with the total population of the greater Durban area it would appear that membership of the new churches comprises a negligible proportion of the total population. However when the growth rate of the new churches is examined, a different picture emerges. For example Durban Christian Centre has grown at a rate of 870 members per year and Pinetown Christian Centre at a rate of 500 members per year. (It must be noted that these figures include children.)

An alternative estimate of membership of the new churches can be derived from the Market Research Africa Survey referred to earlier. Full results can be seen in Appendix 5. When asked to describe their present religious life approximately 2% of the sample said that they were born again Christians in new churches. This is in itself not a large proportion of the population. However a further 2% of the sample said that they were dissatisfied with their older (established) church and interested in a new church like Rhema.

Of the total sample 16% were born-again (8% in established mainline churches, 6% in Pentecostal churches and 2% in new churches), thus confirming that the charismatic movement is strong and well-established. When it is borne in mind that the membership of the new churches comes predominantly from other born-again contexts (see p.114), and from occasional or non-churchgoers (in the MRA survey almost 50% of the total sample), the potential scope for increase in new church membership increases dramatically. Only some 32 percent are regular and satisfied churchgoers in the established mainline churches.

7.5 SERVICES AND SACRAMENTS AND BUILDINGS

Almost all of the new churches hold 2 services on a Sunday. Venues are generally in halls rented for the services, with offices situated in different rented premises. None of the new churches in Durban owns their own premises (bar the Durban Christian Centre which owns the old Lyric theatre and uses it for a Bible College) but most have visions for building their own churches. Only the Pinetown Christian Centre actually owns land for its envisaged church, but others like the Durban Christian Centre have large building funds in readiness.

Holy communion is generally a part of services once a month, and water baptism is conducted on a regular, usually monthly basis. Water baptism is considered to be necessary for attaining the full status of being 'born-again'.

7.6 TRAINING AND ORDINATION OF PASTORS

Some of the new church pastors were already ordained ministers in established churches when they started or joined their particular new churches. It appears that ordination is not as formal as in established churches, the chief concern being a calling from God.

Some of the new church pastors ordained themselves, other co-pastors were ordained by the chief pastor. The training of pastors is considered to be of secondary importance to the 'calling', but it appears that as the new churches are becoming more structured, the training is becoming more formalised.

Rhema Bible Church has a Bible College in Johannesburg where aspirant pastors train before a probationary period when they start a new church or become a co-pastor in an 'established' new church. (Rhema Bible Church also runs its own Bible College in Durban.) The Durban Christian Centre has a Bible College, Christian Bible Training College, where aspirant pastors and others study. The students pay for their own tuition and study full time for 2 years if they want to be pastors. If they have been 'called to the ministry' they become probationary pastors for another 2 years after which their ministry is assessed by experienced 'men of God'. Part time courses are also offered to interested lay persons. Pinetown Christian Centre now also has its own Bible College.

7.7 WOMEN IN LEADERSHIP POSITIONS

The position of women in the new churches is somewhat contradictory. Despite the fact that the new churches subscribe to the belief that women should submit to their husbands, there appears to be little resistance to women being in leadership positions. The wives of pastors are sometimes termed 'co-pastors' or are pastors in their

own right.   The head of the Chatsworth Christian Centre (an out-
reach of the Durban Christian Centre) is a woman and the wives of
pastors regularly lead part of the services.

7.8 POLICY DECISIONS

Policy decisions concerning spiritual matters in the new churches
are made by 'Spiritual Boards', which consist of the pastors and
co-pastors, or if there is only one pastor, the pastor and his
wife.   Some new churches have a board of elders who are in an
advisory capacity particularly regarding finances.   Others, like
Durban Christian Centre, have a Financial Board to advise them on
financial matters.

7.9 FINANCES AND FUNDING

The new churches are, according to their pastors, financed entirely
by love offerings and tithes.   Most have a separate building fund
in preparation for the building of new centres or churches.   A
financial advisor is generally appointed to deal with money matters.

According to one financial advisor who was interviewed:

> - *We run this centre like a business - we have budgets,*
> *forecasts and priorities.   We rate our pastor as the*
> *managing director of a company and pay him accordingly.*
> *He delegates authority to the General Managers (co-*
> *pastors).   Why shouldn't we pay him as much as an MD -*
> *this is a business, God's business, kingdom business.*
> *A worker is worthy of his hire.   It's all in the*
> *contract because we've signed it with God.*

There appears to be little hesitation in discussing fund-raising or
finances, the rationalisation being that large visions for sweeping
revivals need hard cash.   "Rhema has taught South Africa that a
great move of God cannot be financed with jumble sales and morning
markets."   (Channel Jan./Feb. '83, p.21.)

The incomes of the new churches appear to be much higher than the
incomes of established churches of equivalent size although not all

pastors were prepared to divulge budget figures.   Pinetown Christian
Centre with 700 members, has an income of $\pm$ R13 000 per month.
Durban Christian Centre's monthly income (with a membership of 3 000)
is $\pm$ R55 000 with total assets after 4 years of R624 300.

7.10 BUDGETS

New church pastors interviewed were asked what their priorities were
as far as use of funds was concerned.   These were consistently
given as follows:

- salaries

- debts (rental etc.)

- immovable property and building funds

- the needy within the particular body

- evangelists (Christ for all Nations was most often mentioned).

CHAPTER 8

SURVEY FINDINGS AND DISCUSSION OF RESULTS

8.1 SOCIAL DISORGANISATION

To test whether respondents experienced fear and insecurity in relation to the rest of the world, to other people and to the future they were asked to agree or disagree with certain statements. (See Table 2.)

TABLE 2: INSECURITY AND FEARFULNESS

Percentage of respondents in each sample group who agreed with the following statements:

	NCC %	ECC %	MCT %
Today everything in the world is unstable - we should be prepared for constant change, conflict and upheaval	83	90	86
The world is a pretty dangerous place unless one has strong principles	93	90	83
Most people can be trusted	27	55	52
These days a person does not really know who he/she can count on	50	55	34
These days it is difficult to find real friends	37	45	48
It is only natural for me to fear the future in this country	10	65	55
It is only natural for most people to fear the future in this country	79	95	59
	n = 30	n = 20	n = 30

NCC = New church charismatics
ECC = Established church charismatics
MCT = Mainline church traditionalists

Table 2 reveals that the large majority of respondents in all sample groups perceived the world in general as being unstable and dangerous. Clear differences emerged between groups in relation to trusting most

other people. Significantly fewer new church charismatic respondents
felt that most people could be trusted compared with established church
respondents, although they had less difficulty in finding real friends
than established church respondents.

The charismatic sample groups were more unanimous in their belief that
it was difficult to know who could be counted on, revealing a greater
mistrust of people in general than the mainline church traditional
respondents.   Thus, in addition to viewing the world as dangerous and
unstable, the trend was for new church charismatic respondents to be
more suspicious of their fellow human beings than established church
charismatic respondents who were in turn more suspicious than their
mainline church traditional counterparts.

As far as perception of the future in this country was concerned, an
interesting and significant result emerged.   Respondents were asked
to agree or disagree with the following two statements:
  a) It is only natural for me to fear the future in this country.
  b) It is only natural for most people to fear the future
      in this country.

Percentage agreement with the above-mentioned statements a) and b)
was as follows:

	Me	Most	Difference
	%	%	%
New church charismatic respondents	10	79	69
Established church charismatic respondents	65	95	30
Mainline church traditional respondents	55	59	4

It can be inferred from the differences in the percentage of new
church charismatic respondents who agreed that it was only natural
for most people to fear the future in this country (79%) and the
percentage of new church charismatic respondents who agreed that it

was only natural for them to fear the future in this country (10%), that the reason for their lack of fear is because of their member- ship in the new churches. There is a strong possibility that prior to their conversion new church charismatic respondents were just as fearful of the future as they consider other people naturally to be.

In fact during the course of the interviews a number of new church charismatic respondents spontaneously said that they had been fearful prior to conversion.

> -*Before I used to be afraid of death and the future - now I can't wait* (for death) *but we must all go together.*

> -*Before I would have hoped the time bomb would never explode and would have thought of the kids' future - now we pray for our government.*

> -*Before I had a terrible fear - I was really fearful and didn't want to have children in this country. I could see the broken spirits of blacks at my work - now I can see unity in God's love.*

The inference that membership of the new churches is changing peoples' perception of the future is supported by the percentage of established church charismatic respondents who consider it natural for most people to fear the future (95%) compared with the percentage of established church charismatic respondents who consider it natural for themselves to fear the future (65%). Clearly, charismatic churches in general, but new churches particularly, are allaying their members' fears of the future in this country.

As part of the social disorganisation hypothesis it is also necessary to look at the notion of meaningful ties to society. It was hypothesised that the new church charismatic group would, prior to their conversion, have been less involved in any organisations than the other groups and that geographic mobility and job changing could have been a factor in their hypothesised anomic position. It was found that, prior to conversion or 5 years previously, there was no significant difference between the groups in non-religious organisational involvement. (See Table 50, p.191.)

In terms of mobility: job changes, moving house and moving towns, significant differences emerged between the 3 groups. (See Table 3.)

TABLE 3: MOBILITY

Percentage of respondents in each sample group who had, during the past 10 years:

	NCC %	ECC %	MCT %
Changed jobs twice or more than twice	47	15	13
Moved house twice or more than twice	60	25	37
Moved towns once or more than once	43	20	23
	n = 30	n = 20	n = 30

NCC = New church charismatics
ECC = Established church charismatics
MCT = Mainline church traditionalists

Table 3 reveals that significantly more new church charismatic respondents than established church respondents had been mobile in the past 10 years, changing jobs, and moving houses and towns more often than other respondents. Mobility does not necessarily imply insecurity and may, on the contrary, imply confident ambition. It may however indicate fewer supportive networks and a consequent greater need for these, as a contributory factor in joining new churches.

It is hypothesised that the economic insecurity of the present times is pertinent to the growth and success of the new churches. Without a much wider sample one can only speculate that a large percentage of the people attracted to these churches are from precisely that sector of the white population who are most at risk in an economic recession and have the most to lose if customary job reservation is abolished. (See Table 58, p.195 which indicates that a greater percentage of new church charismatic respondents (30%) than other respondents (10%) were people employed in occupations where they were operating for individual profit or commission.)

Respondents were asked to agree or disagree with certain statements
designed to measure economic conservatism (see Table 4), the hypothesis
being that new church charismatics, because of their greater economic
insecurity, would be more conservative than other groups, in terms
of resisting attempts to control the distribution of wealth.

TABLE 4: ECONOMIC ATTITUDES

Percentage of respondents in each sample group who agreed with
the following statements:

	NCC	ECC	MCT
	%	%	%
Large incomes should be taxed much more than they are now, so that everyone can share in the wealth of this land	20	35	17
The incomes of most people are a fair measure of their contribution to the world	27	25	17
Success is mainly due to ability and hard work	70	90	76
Trade unions should become stronger and have more influence generally	13	44	27
It is up to the government to make sure that everyone has a secure job and a good standard of living	43	55	45
If we all received equal salaries, no-one would be motivated to do well	93	80	66
	n = 30	n = 20	n = 30

NCC = New church charismatics
ECC = Established church charismatics
MCT = Mainline church traditionalists

Table 4 reveals that although all groups were economically conservative
on these measures, the trend was for the new church charismatic group
to be most resistant to the suggestion that wealth be redistributed,
confirming the hypothesis that they are economically insecure.

8.2 DEPRIVATION

The economic deprivation theory, as has already been discussed, does
not per se account for the membership of the new churches although
more new church charismatics than other respondents said that they
had experienced financial problems and anxiety about jobs and standard
of living. (See Table 13, p. 84 .)   This is consistent with the
suggestion that the people who are attracted to the new churches may
be economically insecure and perceive themselves as being economically
deprived.

It was hypothesised in the South African context that power or status
deprivation would be a factor in accounting for why people were
attracted to these churches and for what sorts of people were attracted.
The membership composition (see Table 1, p.57) indicates a predominantly
white membership, with a significant Indian and coloured membership.
From observation and from membership figures, very few African
people attend the services.

If the majority of new church members are insecure non-professional
white, Indian and coloured people one can hypothesise that powerlessness is a factor in accounting for their incorporation of the
power of the Holy Spirit, which now gives them some status and
authority in a society/political situation which by and large does
not provide them with a political 'home'.

Some support for the powerlessness hypothesis was obtained from responses to the open-ended question asking people how they felt about
themselves now compared with how they felt about themselves before
they were born-again or 5 years previously (see Table 27, p.129).
Fifty three percent of the new church charismatic respondents said
that they were more confident or had previously lacked confidence
compared with 35 percent of the established church charismatic
respondents and 23 percent of the mainline church traditional
respondents. More significantly, 30 percent of the new church
charismatic respondents said that they now had power/were victorious/
could do whatever they wanted, while neither of the other two groups

made any mention of this fact.

In order to assess whether the attainment of power and control was a significant factor in accounting for the growth and success of the new churches, respondents were asked to agree or disagree with certain statements (see Table 5 below).

TABLE 5: POWERLESSNESS

Percentage of respondents in each sample group who agreed with the following statements:

	NCC	ECC	MCT
	%	%	%
This world is run by the few people in power and there is not much that the ordinary person can do about it	62	75	66
Many times I feel that I have little influence over the things that happen to me	23	40	62
These days one is inclined to give up hope of amounting to something	7	5	10
Sometimes I feel that there is nothing a person like me can do which will make a difference	27	30	52
I am very confident of myself	93	85	70
I have never felt better in my life than I do now	93	75	49
	n = 30	n = 20	n = 30

NCC = new church charismatics
ECC = Established church charismatics
MCT = Mainline church traditionalists

The results indicate that while the majority of all 3 sample groups agree that the world is run by the few people in power and that there is not much the ordinary person can do about it, the charismatic respondents in general perceive themselves as being much less powerless to influence events than the mainline church traditional respondents. Within the charismatic sample, new church charismatic respondents feel

less powerless than the established church charismatic respondents.
Mainline church traditional respondents feel the most powerless
of all respondents.

Clearly charismatic respondents are receiving something in charismatic
churches which is making them feel more in control of their lives and
of events in the world around them.   It is suggested that the power
which is attributed to the infilling of the Holy Spirit, in conjunction
with assurances about the future, are significant factors in accounting
for the power and control which charismatics experience.   The trend
seems to indicate that new churches are enabling people to feel more
powerful than the established charismatic churches or groups, even though
this feeling of power may be essentially illusory.

In terms of organismic deprivation, more new church charismatic respondents than established church respondents said that illness had been
a problem for them before being born-again (see Table 13, p.84).   Confirmation that organismic deprivation could be a factor in accounting
for the growth of charismatic churches was obtained when respondents
were asked to describe the most outstanding miracles which they had
experienced (see Table 26, p.126).   The most common miracle for
both new church charismatic respondents and established church
charismatic respondents was their own personal healing.   The fact
that healing plays such a major part in charismatic churches, particularly the new churches, provides some support for the organismic
deprivation theory.

The psychic deprivation hypothesis (i.e. that people who do not have
meaningful value systems to adhere to are attracted to new religious
movements) is given some support from the church membership histories
of respondents (see Table 6 below).

TABLE 6: DENOMINATIONAL LOYALTY

Percentage of respondents in each sample group who had never changed denominations:

	NCC	ECC	MCT
	%	%	%
	0	25.	60

n = 30 n = 20 n = 30

Number of denominational changes:

	NCC	ECC	MCT
	%	%	%
No change	0	25	60
1 Change	24	38	40
2 Changes	41	16	0
3+ Changes	35	21	0

n = 30 n = 20 n = 30

NCC = New church charismatics
ECC = Established church charismatics
MCT = Mainline church traditionalists

Table 6 reveals that the majority of new·church charismatic respondents (65%) had changed denominations at least twice, with a significant proportion (35%) changing three or more times. These results suggest that the new church charismatic respondents were actually searching for some meaningful set of values which they did not find until they joined their present church. The percentage of established church charismatic respondents who had changed denominations was less than the percentage of new church charismatic respondents who had changed denominations but substantially more than the percentage of mainline church traditional respondents who, if they had changed denominations at all, changed only once. These results seem to suggest that charismatic respondents in general were what they called "seekers": people needing an external, explicit, all-embracing value system.

This is confirmed by the fact that many new church charismatic respondents (57%) volunteered the information that they had been consciously searching for an appropriate church/something as did 33 percent of established church charismatic respondents. Only 17 percent of mainline church traditional respondents said that they had consciously been searching (see Table 49, p.191).

8.3 AUTHORITARIANISM

The hypothesis regarding authoritarianism and related variables was that members of the new churches would be:

more authoritarian

more dogmatic

more intolerant of ambiguity

more reliant on an external source of authority (external locus of control)

than members of the established churches, and that the established church charismatic respondents, because of their adherence to fundamentalist beliefs, would be more authoritarian than the mainline church traditional respondents.

To obtain some measure of authoritarianism and related variables, respondents were asked to agree or disagree with certain statements. (See Tables 7A, B and C below.)

TABLE 7A: AUTHORITARIANISM

Percentage of respondents in each sample group who agreed with the following statements:

	NCC %	ECC %	MCT %
A few good strong leaders would make this country better than all the laws and talk	60	70	59
It is difficult for me to take orders and do what I am told	17	21	28
Maintenance of law and order in this country is more important than freedom for all	69	55	55
Obedience and respect for authority are the most important virtues that children should learn	90	80	52
The general public is not qualified to vote on today's complex issues	60	50	59
	n = 30	n = 20	n = 30

NCC = New church charismatics
ECC = Established church charismatics
MCT = Mainline church traditionalists

The item which most strongly differentiated between the three groups was "Obedience and respect for authority are the most important virtues that children should learn". Here there was far more consensus amongst new church charismatic respondents and established church charismatic respondents, giving support to the hypothesis that a fundamentalist orientation encourages authoritarian submission.

The statements which were intended to measure whether respondents were reliant on an external source of authority revealed a far greater similarity between charismatic respondents than between either of these groups and mainline church traditional respondents. The hypothesis that a fundamentalist orientation fosters reliance on an external locus of control was supported by responses to statements in Table 7B.

TABLE 7B: EXTERNAL LOCUS OF CONTROL

Percentage of respondents in each sample group who agreed with the following statements:

	NCC %	ECC %	MCT %
On our own as individuals we cannot find direction and meaning in life	70	65	48
It is a great relief to have handed over all my worries and decisions to the Lord	93	80	40
In this complicated world of ours, the only way we can know what is going on is to rely on leaders or experts who can be trusted	57	50	66
	n = 30	n = 20	n = 30

NCC = New church charismatics
ECC = Established church charismatics
MCT = Mainline church traditionalists

The same statements were used to measure both dogmatism and intolerance of ambiguity (see Table 7C below) and for these statements the difference between the charismatics and traditionals was significantly marked.

TABLE 7C: DOGMATISM

Percentage of respondents in each sample group who agreed with the following statements:

	NCC %	ECC %	MCT %
The only way to make sure that things get done right is to set up a definite and fixed schedule and never depart from it	60	55	34
When all is said and done, simple truths have more to offer than all the theories in Science and education	100	85	52
Once a person makes up his/her mind about something he/she should stick to his/her conclusion instead of repeatedly rehashing the question	83	90	38
It is the devil who plants doubt and un- certainty in peoples' minds	100	100	33
	n = 30	n = 20	n = 30

NCC = New church charismatics
ECC = Established church charismatics
MCT = Mainline church traditionalists

It is clear from these results that the charismatic group generally are far more certain of their beliefs than the mainline church traditional respondents and that, in terms of the variables mentioned, they are more dogmatic and intolerant of ambiguity than the mainline church traditional respondents. Within the charismatic group, new church charismatics are more dogmatic and intolerant of ambiguity than the established church charismatic respondents. It becomes clear from responses to the following statement:

"It is the devil who plants doubt and uncertainty in peoples' minds."

Percentage agreement

NCC %	ECC %	MCT %
100	100	33

that the charismatic respondents are not only intolerant of ambiguity but positively aver it as being of the devil. On its own this finding

may appear to be relatively innocuous, but in conjunction with authoritarianism and a great reliance on an external source of authority, it
has serious implications for the power which the leaders and teachings
of the new churches have, if not in reality then potentially.

Members of the new churches are taught that doubt and uncertainty are
Satanic, and that obedience and respect for authority are paramount
virtues. Within this framework there would appear to be no mechanisms
or strategies for members to critically examine anything that they are
told.

In the new churches criticism and uncertainty are pre-empted in two
ways: members are told that they will experience doubts and when they
do they will know that the devil and his forces are at work; members
are told that everything that is said and taught in the new churches
has Biblical support. Isolated verses are often read out in services
to substantiate statements. The interviewers experienced this method
of substantiation constantly during interviews, with new church respondents
quoting isolated Biblical verses. Exegesis does not appear to be
particularly strong in the new churches: the fact that something is
written in the Bible, no matter what its context, is deemed to be
sufficient proof of its validity.

An interesting circumvention of the Bible as the only source of authority
is found in the new churches' literature and during sermons. To substantiate some fresh insight that is not from the Bible, pastors and
authors simply claim direct revelation from God.

An example of the authority structure conceived of by the new churches
and which must severely repress, if not preclude questioning, is found
in the organisational chart of Rhema Bible Church, Johannesburg.

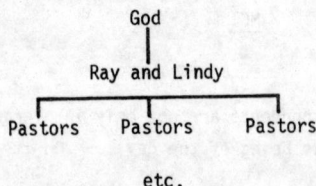

```
                    God
                     |
                Ray and Lindy
        ┌────────────┼────────────┐
     Pastors      Pastors      Pastors

                    etc.
```

8.4 POLITICAL CONSERVATISM AND INVOLVEMENT

Political conservatism is closely allied with authoritarianism as it is with adherence to conservative churches. Voting patterns (see Table 8A below) indicate that new church charismatic respondents are more politically conservative than established church respondents. The fact that far more new church charismatic respondents than other respondents do not vote at all and are not interested in politics (see Table 8A, B and C below) confirms the contention that passivity amounts to support of the status quo.

TABLE 8: POLITICAL PARTICIPATION

8A: VOTING

Percentage of respondents in each sample group who said they voted for the following parties:

	NCC	ECC	MCT
	%	%	%
Nationalist or Conservative	53	35	17
NRP	13	30	23
PFP	13	35	50
None	20	0	10

8B: POLITICAL INTEREST

Percentage of respondents in each sample group who agreed with the following statements:

	NCC	ECC	MCT
	%	%	%
I am really interested in the differences between the political parties	23	40	59
A sensible person should mind his/her own business and not concern him/herself about politics	57	30	21
It is essential to vote when there is a general election	90	75	86

8C: SPONTANEOUS MENTION OF POLITICAL INTEREST

Percentage of respondents in each sample group who spontaneously gave the following responses to open-ended questions concerning political attitudes:

	NCC	ECC	MCT
	%	%	%
Have never been interested in politics	76	47	39
Used to be interested in politics but now not interested	14	0	0
Therefore total percentage who stated present lack of interest	90	47	39

n = 30 n = 20 n = 30

NCC = New church charismatics
ECC = Established church charismatics
MCT = Mainline church traditionalists

Although new church charismatic respondents evinced much less interest
in politics than other respondents this did not extend to voting.
The large majority of all respondents agreed that it was essential to
vote, although 20 percent of new church charismatic respondents did
not in fact vote. The concern with voting could merely be a reflection
of conformity, however.

Table 9 illustrates that new church charismatics are more acquiescent
and willing to support the government than other respondents.

TABLE 9:   POLITICAL ATTITUDES

Percentage of respondents in each sample group who agreed with
the following statements:

	NCC %	ECC %	MCT %
We should submit to those placed in authority over us without question (governments)	73	55	10
The only way this country and the world will come right is through prayer and the spreading of the gospel	100	95	62
Conscientious objectors are traitors to their country	55	15	28
We should be willing to fight for our country without question	77	55	38
Detention without trial should be abolished in this country	76	79	83
	n = 30	n = 20	n = 30

NCC = New church charismatics
ECC = Established church charismatics
MCT = Mainline church traditionalists

Table 9 illustrates that new church charismatic respondents are much
more willing to fight for this country at the present time than other
respondents.   The majority of new church charismatic respondents
(73%) believed in submission without question to governments in
authority, as did more than half (55%) of the established church
charismatic respondents.   Only 10 percent of mainline church
traditional respondents believed this to be true.   A notable and
unpredictable result was obtained regarding respondents' attitudes

towards dention without trial. All three sample groups strongly
disagreed with this and felt that it should be abolished. This is
only to be expected, however - few people can be expected to overtly
agree with inroads into the rule of law.

8.4.1. Racial attitudes

The new churches are avowedly non-racial and services are not re-
stricted to any particular race group. It was however suggested
that in line with greater authoritarianism and political conservatism
new church charismatics would be more racist than other respondents
and that established church charismatics would be more racist than
mainline church traditionalists. Table 10 results suggest that
this may well be the case.

TABLE 10: RACIAL ATTITUDES

Percentage of respondents in each sample group who agreed with the
following statements:

	NCC	ECC	MCT
	%	%	%
It would be acceptable for me have a coloured foreman supervising whites	86	95	97
All forms of racial discrimination should be made illegal	54	65	76
I would willingly admit blacks to my church or club as personal friends	87	90	80
If it is well-planned, there is nothing wrong with black pupils being admitted to white schools	64	95	79
If neighbourhood standards did not drop, I would be quite happy to have African people living in my street as neighbours	59	65	62
There may be a few exceptions, but in general Indians are pretty much alike	57	40	28
I think mixed marriages between races should be strongly discouraged	73	65	62
One way or another all races and creeds should have the right to vote for our parliament	46	60	76
Newspapers exaggerate about the condition of blacks in this country	79	60	45
Unfortunately it seems that now that blacks have taken over, Zimbabwe has much less chance of making progress	69	75	59
Apartheid is a sin	47	55	62

n = 30 n = 20 n = 30

NCC = New church charismatics
ECC = Established church charismatics
MCT = Mainline church traditionalists

It must be noted that on certain of the statements intended to measure
racial attitudes, none of the sample groups was found to be particularly
racist, although some of the statements were phrased in such a manner
that the reasonable response was to be non-racist and the statements
should perhaps have been more challenging.

For example the majority of all groups found it (in decreasing order
of popularity), acceptable to have a coloured foreman supervising
whites, would willingly admit blacks to their church or club as
personal friends, would willingly admit black pupils to white schools
(if it was well-planned) and would willingly have African people living
in their streets as neighbours (if neighbourhood standards did not
drop). It must be noted however that fewer new church charismatic
respondents than other respondents agreed with the above statements
except for admitting blacks to their church or club. This is in
line with the new churches' teaching that Christians are all equal
in the eyes of God. *"We even embrace them you know"*, a typical
response in support of new church charismatic respondents' claims
to non-racism, is indicative of the inconsistency in this attitude.

These 'non-racist' findings are confusing in view of the fact that
the majority of the new church charismatic and one third of established
church charismatic respondents vote Nationalist. Either their apparent
lack of racism means that they do not know what the Nationalist
party actually stands for and are voting contrary to their true feelings regarding race matters or, more likely, they are mouthing plat-
itudes and paying lip-service to non-racialism in the secure knowledge
that the envisaged changes are nowhere near reality.

The ethnocentrism of all three groups was clearly evident in their
response to the statement 'Mixed marriages should be strongly discouraged'. The new church charismatic group was most in favour of
this statement (73%) followed by the established church charismatic
respondents (65%) with the mainline church traditional respondents
least in favour (62%). Racism was also evident in response to the
statement that Zimbabwe has much less chance of making progress now

that blacks have taken over.   More than 50 percent of all three groups
agreed with this statement.

Clearer differences began to emerge between sample groups in their
attitudes towards the following: more than half the new church charismatic group felt that Indians were pretty much alike as opposed to 40
percent of established church charismatics and only 27 percent of
mainline church traditionalists.   The new church charismatic group
felt very strongly (79%) that newspapers exaggerate about the
condition of blacks in this country while 45 percent of mainline
church traditionalists felt this.   The new church charismatic respondents (54%) were also less keen than other respondents that all forms
of racial discrimination should be made illegal.

Responses to the statement 'Apartheid is a sin' seemed to cause some
confusion to many respondents.   A notable percentage of all respondents said they were uncertain about this (25% of the total sample),
and many people voiced confusion over what was meant by 'apartheid'.
It seems that many people chose to understand this to mean petty
apartheid as opposed to the policy of separate development. Nevertheless the trend follows the predictable pattern of new church
charismatics being most conservative followed by establish church
charismatics, with mainline church traditionalists being least conservative.

Percentage agreement with the statement: Apartheid is a sin

NCC	ECC	MCT
%	%	%
47	55	62

8.4.2 Changes in political attitudes

The question still remains as to whether the political views held by
new church respondents existed prior to their conversion or whether
they exist as a result of their conversion to the new churches and
whether the new churches are influencing members' political attitudes
(see Tables 11 and 12).

TABLE 11: CHANGES IN POLITICAL ATTITUDES

Percentage of respondents in each sample group who agreed that
their political attitudes had changed since being born-again/
in the last 5 years:

	NCC	ECC	MCT
	%	%	%
	66	55	30

SPONTANEOUS REPLIES

Percentage of respondents in each sample group whose political
attitudes had changed in the following ways:

	NCC	ECC	MCT
	%	%	%
Never interested in politics but support government	54	25	17
Used to be anti-government but now support it or understand it better	15	15	4
Never interested in politics but anti-government	20	10	13
Used to be pro-government but now anti	4	20	8
Always been anti-government	7	30	58
	n = 30	n = 20	n = 30

NCC = New church charismatics
ECC = Established church charismatics
MCT = Mainline church traditionalists

TABLE 12: CHANGES IN RACIAL ATTITUDES - SPONTANEOUS MENTION

Percentage of respondents in each sample group who spontaneously said
the following concerning racial attitudes:

	NCC	ECC	MCT
	%	%	%
Remained the same (or did not mention race)	27	50	88
Become more tolerant though never previously racist	30	25	3
Become more tolerant - previously disliked blacks	10	0	3
All people are equal in the eyes of God	20	5	0
Become more aware of problems of blacks	13	20	6
	n = 30	n = 20	n = 30

NCC = New church charismatics
ECC = Established church charismatics
MCT = Mainline church traditionalists

Table 11 reveals that more than half of the charismatic respondents
(66% of new church charismatics and 55% of established church charismatics) said that their political attitudes had changed since being
born-again compared with 30 percent of mainline church traditionalists
who said that their political attitudes had changed in the last 5 years.
This supports the contention that charismatic Christianity in general
and new churches in particular are actively influencing the political
attitudes and behaviour of their adherents.

Fifteen percent of both charismatic groups said that they had previously been anti-government but now supported it or understood it
better compared with only 4 percent of mainline church traditionalists
who said this.   Only 4 percent of new church charismatics said that
they had changed in the direction of being more anti-government compared with 20 percent of established church charismatics and 8 percent
of mainline church traditionalists.   Becoming more pro-government is
the most common change for new church charismatics the majority of
whom are pro-government, while becoming more anti-government is the
most common change for established church respondents, the majority
of whom are anti-government.

Most of the stated changes in political attitudes were in the area
of apparently increased racial tolerance of new church charismatic
respondents (see Table 12).

The following comments from new church charismatic respondents give
some indication of the kind of changes experienced in the area of
racial tolerance:

- *Before I hated blacks - now I know that it's nothing
  to do with the colour of skin.*
- *I've softened a lot - ah - I couldn't handle the munts
  before, I used to swat coons and that.   Now it doesn't
  hassle me.   I can see why they're like that - they
  haven't got salvation.*
- *People are so full of bitterness and resentment -
  unless Christ is there to take it out you can't mix.*

- *Indian and African churches are linked to the Durban
  Christian Centre and this helps in the mixing of races.*
- *I have more love for blacks than I ever did.*
- *Hindus - if you're not preaching to them you shouldn't
  mix with them. If I was surrounded by Hindus I would
  be worried - demons all around me. Immediately you
  go into Chatsworth you can feel the evil spirits
  tangibly on you.*
- *I've become aware that a lot of prayer is needed for
  our nation - through mixed meetings at church I hear
  black people witness - they tell you that they haven't
  loved you. This gives you a shock.*
- *People get set free from bondages - depression, race
  hatred, despondency - e.g. an Indian man wept when a
  white woman held his hand - it's too beautiful man.
  An Afrikaner started weeping when he held hands with
  a black.*

It seems, according to voting patterns, that increased racial tolerance
does not in any way imply a consequent condemnation of or opposition
to the notion of 'separate development', but rather an anti-petty
apartheid stance along with an ephemeral equality in the eyes of God.

8.5 PERSONALITY TYPES AND LIFE CRISES

It is difficult to ascertain what people were like prior to an experience that has fundamentally altered their perceptions of themselves, and of the world around them. There is also considerable difficulty and danger in attempting to separate individual personality factors from the society in which they are situated. Within the constraints of the above-mentioned problems, the following picture (see Table 13) emerged when respondents were asked whether certain problems (some of which have already been referred to) had seriously applied to them before they were born-again/five or more years previously:

TABLE 13: LIFE CRISES

Percentage of respondents in each sample group who agreed that they had experienced the following problems before being born-again or 5 or more years previously:

	NCC	ECC	MCT
	% *	% *	% *
Financial problems	57	10	23
Anxiety about standard of living	53	20	37
Anxiety about the future	50	50	46
Marital problems	50	30	30
Depression	47	40	40
Illness	47	30	30
Death of a close person	43	45	67
Anxiety about job	38	20	33
Alcohol problems	30	15	26
Demonic problems	17	0	0
Other problems	30	25	20

Percentage of respondents in each sample group who agreed that the following problems applied to them at present:

	NCC	ECC	MCT
	% *	% *	% *
Financial problems	10	5	7
Anxiety about standard of living	10	0	7
Anxiety about the future	7	15	23
Marital problems	10	5	10
Depression	20	10	10
Illness	10	15	13
Death of a close person	3	0	10
Anxiety about job	10	5	7
Alcohol problems	0	0	10
Demonic problems	7	0	0
Other problems	7	10	7
	n = 30	n = 20	n = 30

NCC = New church charismatics
ECC = Established church charismatics
MCT = Mainline church traditionalists

* Respondents could give more than one response

These results indicate that more new church charismatic respondents
than established church respondents experienced all the problems mentioned except for the death of a close person.   This finding provides
some support for the hypothesis that people attracted to new religious
movements are more likely to have experienced personality problems or
life crises, which would be contributory factors in their conversion
to the new churches.

Table 56 (p.194) reveals that 20 percent of the new church charismatic
respondents were divorced compared with none of the established church
charismatics and 7 percent of the mainline church traditional respondents.   While acknowledging that the sampling method could have
contributed to this finding, it is suggested that the trauma of a
divorce is likely to encourage conversion to a warm, emotional, total
commitment group.

During the course of the interviews all charismatic respondents gave
their testimonies one way or another, despite the fact that they were
not specifically asked for them.   The interviewers, on the basis of
these testimonies, noted what they considered the chief influences in
the respondents' conversions to be.   Of the 30 new church charismatics
interviewed 13 (i.e. 43%) had had serious problems according to their
testimonies.   A brief summary of some of the testimonies provides some
support for the personality/life crises hypothesis:

Respondent A:	Married at 17, 4 children in rapid succession, husband an alcoholic, husband left - attempted suicide - friends took her to a Pentecostal church.
Respondent B:	Suffered from severe eczema, stomach complaint, in therapy with a psychologist - too scared to have children because of the situation in South Africa - divorced - chance meeting led her to a Christian Centre.
Respondent C:	Alcoholic - nervous breakdown - admitted to psychiatric hospital - divorced - chance meeting

led him to a Christian Centre.

Of the 20 established church charismatic respondents interviewed 3 (i.e. 15%) had had serious problems according to their testimonies.   They were more likely than new church charismatic respondents to have become born-again due to the charismatic movements within their churches or through being brought up in a Pentecostal church.   (See Table 53 p.193 and Table 22 p.113.)

The most common problems experienced by new church charismatic respondents prior to conversion were:
  - financial problems

  - anxiety about maintaining a decent standard of living

  - anxiety about the future.

For the established church charismatic respondents the most common problems experienced prior to conversion were:
  - anxiety about the future

  - death of a close person

  - depression

For mainline church traditional respondents the most common problems experienced 5 or more years previously were:
  - death of a close person

  - anxiety about the future

  - depression

In terms of the most common problems for each group, it is interesting to note that while death, the future and depression were the most common problems for the mainline church traditional and established church charismatic respondents, financial problems, anxiety about standard of living and anxiety about the future were most common for the new church charismatic respondents.

The problems which differentiated new church charismatic respondents

most significantly from other respondents were: financial problems,
anxiety about maintaining a decent standard of living and marital
problems. The emphasis on problems relating to money could indicate
that new church charismatic respondents are less secure financially,
perhaps because they are more likely to be in occupations which are
at risk i.e. non-professional jobs which would be threatened by the
abolition of job reservation, or sales jobs which depend upon com-
petition with other sales people.

When asked which problems applied to them now, respondents in all
three groups said they had fewer problems now than prior to being born-
again/five or more years previously. This may indicate an understandable reluctance on the part of the respondents to divulge painful
present personal difficulties if any did exist. Also one must assume
a greater reticence on the part of charismatic respondents in general
to admit to problems when their problems should have been overcome.
Bearing these reservations in mind, the only problems which were
significantly different between sample groups were: depression
(more of the new church charismatic respondents said that depression
was presently a problem than other respondents), and anxiety about the
future which was presently a problem for more mainline church traditional
respondents than other respondents. The fact that more mainline
church traditional respondents are at present fearful of the future
confirms that charismatic religion in general is somehow allaying
members' fears.

In an attempt to discover whether new church charismatics were more
anxious than other respondents prior to conversion and what their
present level of anxiety was, respondents were asked to agree or
disagree with the statements in Table 14 (below).

TABLE 14: ANXIETY

Percentage of respondents in each sample group who agreed with
the following statements:

	NCC %	ECC %	MCT %
In the past I certainly had more than my fair share of things to worry about	63	45	41
I often find myself worrying about something or someone	30	65	86
	n = 30	n = 20	n = 30

NCC = New church charismatics
ECC = Established church charismatics
MCT = Mainline church traditionalists

Significantly more new church charismatic respondents felt that they
had had more than their fair share of things to worry about in the
past, while their present level of anxiety was considerably lower
than established church charismatic respondents and very much lower
than mainline church traditional respondents (86 % of whom
presently often worry about something or someone).   New church
charismatic respondents appear, prior to conversion, to have been
more anxious than other respondents, but are now much less anxious
than other respondents.

This finding is confirmed by responses to the open-ended question
concerning personal changes as a result of conversion (see Table
27, p.129).   Significantly more charismatics (30 % of new church
charismatics and 25 % of established church charismatics) than
mainline church traditionalists (7%) said that they were presently
less anxious than they had been prior to conversion or 5 or more
years previously.

These findings regarding present and past anxieties appear to confirm
the suggestion that charismatic churches in general, but particularly
new churches, are relieving the anxiety of their members who, it is
suggested, were more anxious than normal prior to joining these churches.

Some support for the suggestion that new church charismatic respondents were in fact more anxious than others prior to conversion was obtained from spontaneous remarks by new church charismatic respondents:

- *Before I had fear right here in my stomach - I used to fear my work and got over it through drinking.*
- *I used to go to work in a state of terror - a knot of terror, wondering what was going to go wrong.*
- *Before I was fear ridden - if I went into a shop the perspiration just ran.*
- *I was tormented in the past - worrying about everything.*

No such comments were made by other respondents.

8.5.1 Dealing with problems: Satanic solutions

The new church pastors were asked what sorts of problems people came to them with. Their replies in combination were: marital problems, communication problems, financial problems, unemployment problems, guilt, depression, inadequacy, illness and occult problems. Apart from occult problems it seems likely that these problems would be commonly encountered by any clergy of any denomination.

The frequent mention by new church pastors of occult problems indicates the emphasis in new church teachings on the Satanic origin of many problems. Apart from attributing poverty and illness to Satan, psychological problems are also attributed to Satan either directly or indirectly. The following were typical responses from pastors in this regard:

- *People can have psychological problems but these are demonic if the person has opened the door to the devil. You can tell that a person is oppressed by demons when he seems driven and has no control in sex and eating for example.*
- *Satan is the instigator and motivator of psychological problems.*

Although only 20 percent of new church charismatic respondents said

that they had experienced demonic problems or occult involvement,
(see Table 13, p.84), 50 percent of new church charismatic respondents spontaneously mentioned Satanic intervention in their lives
during the course of the interviews.

Of the new church charismatic respondents who mentioned Satanic
intervention in their lives:

>   20 percent believed they had been personally possessed or
>   oppressed by demons and had had exorcism performed on them.

>   20 percent believed they had experienced evil spirits and
>   had personally rebuked them.

>   60 percent stated that Satan had particularly or generally
>   tried to undermine them.

The vast majority of new church respondents believe that the devil causes
psychological problems (see Table 20, p.105) and that the devil puts
doubt and uncertainty in peoples' minds.   Bearing this in mind one must
allow for the possibility that when new church charismatics do experience psychological problems they attribute these to Satan and do
not endeavour to resolve these problems by rational confrontation
but repress them.   This casts some doubt on the validity of the
findings that very few new church charismatic respondents presently
admit to experiencing any problems at all.

The implication that psychological problems are attributed to Satan and
repressed was confirmed by responses from new church charismatic respondents:

- *Sometimes I still get depressed but I pray about it
  and command it to leave.*
- *When I doubt I know who it is - Satan.*
- *The dizzy spell goes over when I speak in tongues -
  I just rebuke it and start praising God.*
- *Now when I get depressed I sing a praise or hum a
  tune.*

Exorcism is practised by the new churches, if demonic spirits have been discerned.

It is of some concern to psychologists that psychological problems are being dealt with in this manner. A psychologist interviewed during this survey referred to a case in which a young person bordering on severe psychosis was told by a new church Pastor that he was oppressed by demons. An exorcism followed which appeared to precipitate a severe psychotic breakdown. The psychologist concerned was not prepared to say that the exorcism had caused the psychotic breakdown but did say that it was a contributory factor. The consensus amongst his colleagues was that it was extremely dangerous and potentially harmful for people unfamiliar with the various manifestations of psychopathology to intervene in the dramatic form which exorcism takes.

New church pastors were asked how they normally dealt with psychological problems. Generally, the first step was to make sure the person was born-again after which the problems were easily solved by using 'the Word'; counselling them to have faith in what God had done for them and what God's promises were for them. The pastors were critical of the way in which established church ministers dealt with problems, saying that they simply told people to take courage and have faith without showing them how to have faith.

Established church ministers interviewed were, on the other hand, critical of the new church pastors' methods of counselling. They spoke of having to cope with the 'casualties' of the new churches: people who had been told that the reason for their illness, death of a loved one, or psychological problems was that they had not had enough faith or that they were allowing Satan to dominate and oppress them.

It seems that the teachings of the new churches are encouraging members to perceive their problems and failure to solve them as being purely Satanic in origin. Proof of this contention was obtained when 100 percent of all charismatics agreed that it was the "devil who plants

doubt and uncertainty in peoples' minds". (See Table 7C, p.74.)
New church charismatic respondents also spontaneously offered the
following comments prior to being asked about Satan.

- *The symptoms came back 2 weeks later and I knew it
  was Satan trying to rob me.*
- *Everything that you fear will come onto you - the
  devil's making you fear things.*
- *The devil comes up against you and makes you feel
  worthless.*
- *I knew it was Satan trying to rob me.*
- *The devil tried to get me to commit suicide.*
- *If you don't bump into him it means you're going along
  with him.*

8.6 PERCEPTION OF THE CHURCH'S FUNCTION

Respondents were read a list of potential church tasks and asked to
rate them as being of great importance, fairly important, unimportant
or nothing to do with the church (see Table 16, p.96 below). The
tasks ranged from the most obvious (winning people to Christ) to the
most contentious (actively working for political and social justice).

From the graph (see Graph 1, p.97 below) it can be seen that there
was complete consensus on certain church functions: winning people
to Christ, giving Bible instruction, getting back to simple Bible
truths, providing fellowship and a sense of belonging, ministering
to and helping people with their problems, and helping the needy.

There was almost complete consensus on the importance of the following
functions: giving inspiration and joy in worship, teaching meekness
and humility, and giving clear answers in this complex modern world.
(See Table 16.)   The trend clearly confirms Kelley's (1977) theory
that the primary task of a church is to provide for members' individual
needs for meaning and belonging.   All groups consistently rated the
social justice functions of the church as being less important than
the 'primary' functions.

However, it is clear from the graph that the new church charismatic
group attribute the least importance and object most strongly to
the church involving itself with issues of social justice.   This
is most clearly illustrated by the percentage of responses in the
strongest negative category "nothing to do with church" (see Table
15 below).

TABLE 15: ATTITUDES TOWARDS THE SOCIAL GOSPEL

Percentage of respondents who said that the following tasks had
nothing to do with the church:

	NCC	ECC	MCT
	%	%	%
Working for the equality of all people	40	20	13
Actively working for political and social justice for all	67	45	43
Teaching the congregations about the injustices in this country	77	45	40
Urging the government to abandon apartheid as unChristian	83	45	37
	n = 30	n = 20	n = 30

NCC = New church charismatics
ECC = Established church charismatics
MCT = Mainline church traditionalists

Other church tasks about which there was considerable disagreement
were: providing signs and wonders and miracles, teaching the need
for self-discipline hard work and duty, helping people to succeed
and prosper, and preserving traditional forms of worship.

It is to be expected from the emphasis in the new churches, and the
charismatic movement in general, on manifestations of God's power,
that the new church charismatics and established church charismatics
rate signs and wonders and miracles far more highly than the mainline
church traditionalists. It is important to note and consistent
with the new churches' teachings on prosperity that the new church
charismatics rate "Helping people to succeed and prosper" as highly
as they rate the 'primary' tasks of the church.

The disparity amongst the groups on the "self-discipline, hard work
and duty" item is consistent with the fundamentalist orientation of
the new churches and may confirm the theory that new churches/sects
facilitate upward mobility by inculcating the attributes which promote
success in our kind of society.

It is predictable that mainline church traditionalists and established church charismatics would rate "Preserving traditional forms of worship" more highly than the new church charismatics in view of the fact that the new churches decry traditional worship as stultifying or dead.

TABLE 16: IMPORTANCE OF CHURCH TASKS

Percentage of respondents in each sample group who said that it was a) of great or fair importance that the church should perform the following tasks b) that these tasks were unimportant or nothing to do with the church:

	Great/fair importance			Unimportant/ not church		
	NCC %	ECC %	MCT %	NCC %	ECC %	MCT %
Winning people to Christ	100	100	100	0	0	0
Giving Bible instruction	100	100	100	0	0	0
Getting back to simple Bible truths	100	100	100	0	0	0
Providing fellowship and a sense of belonging	100	100	100	0	0	0
Ministering to and helping people with their problems	100	100	100	0	0	0
Helping the needy	100	100	100	0	0	0
Giving inspiration and joy in worship	100	95	93	0	5	7
Helping people overcome fear and anxiety	100	100	87	0	0	13
Providing freedom of worship	100	95	83	0	5	17
Teaching the need for self-discipline, hard work and duty	97	55	67	3	45	33
Teaching meekness and humility	93	90	87	7	10	13
Giving clear answers in this complex modern world	90	85	80	10	15	20
Helping people to succeed and prosper	97	55	33	3	45	67
Providing signs and wonders and miracles	93	75	23	7	25	77
Working for the equality of all people	53	65	77	47	35	23
Actively working for political and social justice for all	23	35	53	77	65	47
Teaching the congregations about the injustices in this country	17	30	47	83	70	53
Urging the government to abandon apartheid as unChristian	13	35	50	87	65	50
Preserving traditional forms of worship	7	55	57	93	45	43
	n = 30	n = 20	n = 30	n = 30	n = 20	n = 30

NCC = New church charismatics
ECC = Established church charismatics
MCT = Mainline church traditionalists

GRAPH 1: RELATIVE IMPORTANCE OF CHURCH TASKS

Frequency distribution showing percentage respondents in each sample group who said that it was important for the church to undertake certain tasks (the full list can be seen on p.94.)

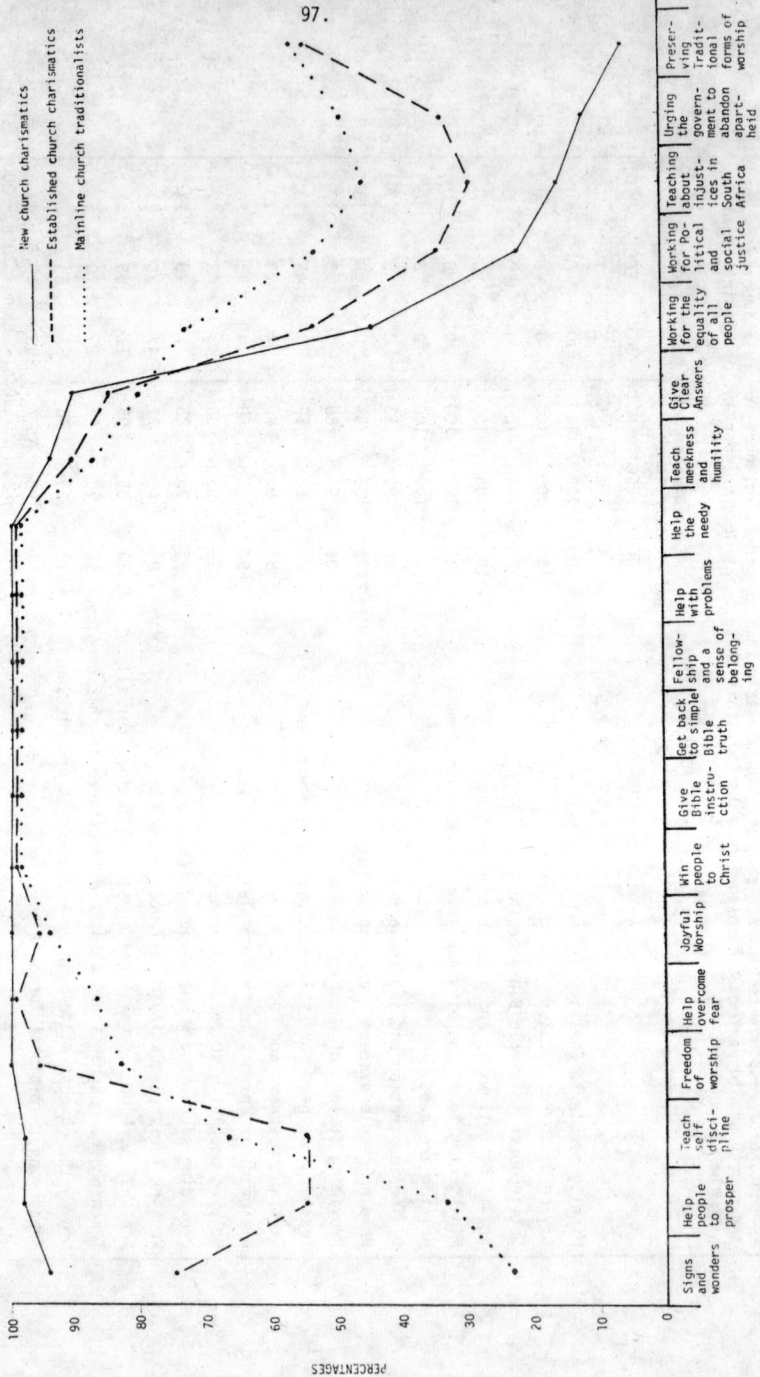

New church charismatics
Established church charismatics
Mainline church traditionalists

PERCENTAGES

100 90 80 70 60 50 40 30 20 10 0

Signs and wonders
Help people to prosper
Teach self-discipline
Freedom of worship
Help overcome fear
Joyful Worship
Win people to Christ
Give Bible instruction
Get back to simple Bible truth
Fellowship and a sense of belonging
Help with problems
Help the needy
Teach meekness and humility
Give Clear Answers
Working for the equality of all people
Working for political and social justice
Teaching about injustices in South Africa
Urging the government to abandon apartheid
Preserving traditional forms of worship

8.6.1 Perception of the duties of individual Christians

Respondents were asked about different aspects of Christian behaviour
in terms of whether they agreed, disagreed or were uncertain about
whether such aspects were intrinsic to being a Christian.

TABLE 17: DUTIES OF INDIVIDUAL CHRISTIANS

Percentage of respondents in each sample group who agreed that
Christian individuals should, because they were Christians, do
the following:

	NCC	ECC	MCT
	%	%	%
Live a life of devoted prayer, Bible study and worship	100	95	53
Be a community of persons who know and care for one another	97	95	87
Be active in proclaiming the gospel to other individuals	93	100	53
Work for racial harmony and reconciliation between individuals	43	60	70
Be involved in community welfare projects for the less privileged	40	50	70
Be mainly concerned for the needs of their own individual parish	30	25	23
Actively work for social justice	20	35	47
Be mainly concerned with the most urgent social, political and economic problems of society	3	10	23
	n = 30	n = 20	n = 30

NCC = New church charismatics
ECC = Established church charismatics
MCT = Mainline church traditionalists

For this question the priorities given by the new church charismatic
and established church charismatic respondents were quite different
from those given by the mainline church traditional respondents, the
only similarity being that all groups agreed that being a community

of persons who knew and cared for one another was a top priority.
Otherwise both new church charismatic and established church charismatic
respondents agreed consistently that living a life of devoted prayer,
Bible study and worship , and being active in proclaiming the gospel
to other individuals were the most important activities for Christian
individuals to be engaged in.   This is consistent with the conservative
evangelical stance of the new churches and the older Pentecostal churches.

The mainline church traditional respondents, on the other hand, were
most unanimous that being involved in community welfare projects and
working for racial harmony and reconciliation between individuals
were the most important activities.   This finding (to some extent)
contradicts the trend for all groups on their perceptions of what
the church should be doing, and it can be inferred from this that
while the mainline church traditional group did not consider these
to be top priorities for the church as a whole they did consider
them to be necessary for individual Christians to do.

All three groups rated actively working for social justice as being
relatively unimportant but 47 percent of the new church charismatic
group as opposed to only 27 percent of the mainline church traditional
group firmly disagreed that this was intrinsic to being a Christian.

All three groups rated concern with the needs of their own individual
parishes as being very unimportant.   This is significant in view of
the fact that the new churches promote so-called non-denominationalism,
and condemn the factionalism of the mainline churches.

8.7 ABSOLUTE ANSWERS

Social disorganisation theory suggests that fundamentalist evangelical
churches appeal in times of stress and insecurity because they offer
absolute answers.   Kelley (1977) within a different framework, contends
that churches which dispense meaning most effectively will flourish and
grow.   The effective dispensing of meaning for Kelley necessitates
authoritarian features like absolutism, discipline, conformity and
fanaticism.

We have seen that all respondents in the sample thought it imperative
that the church should get back to simple Bible truths and that most
respondents thought it important that the church should provide clear
answers in this complex modern world.   Our contention is that part
of the appeal of the new churches is that they do provide absolute
answers in simple, contemporary language.   An examination of some
of the absolute answers provided by the new churches is therefore
necessary and illuminating.

8.7.1 Fundamentalism and absolutism

Most new church pastors interviewed said that they had answers to
every question that could be posed and that these answers were to be
found in the Bible, which is literally interpreted.   According to
the new churches, salvation is only for born-again Christians.   Heaven
and hell are real places.   The devil and his princes are at work and
their principalities are real.   Christians should submit to those
placed in authority over them without question to avoid the doubt
and confusion of the Devil.

To test whether respondents accepted and adhered to these beliefs they
were asked to agree or disagree with certain statements.   (See Table
18 below.)

TABLE 18: CONSERVATIVE FUNDAMENTALISM

Percentage of respondents in each sample group who agreed with the following statements:

	NCC %	ECC %	MCT %
I believe that all of the Bible is inspired by God and is literally true	93	90	30
There is no such thing as a physical hell where men are punished after death for their sins	7	10	47
I believe there is a supernatural being, the devil, who continually tries to lead people into sin	100	100	47
A child is not born into the world already guilty of sin	17	30	60
In the world today, people like me can be persecuted for religious beliefs	95	95	50
Eternal life is not only for born-again Christians	3	30	80
A practising religious Hindu could gain eternal life	3	10	38
We should submit to those placed in authority over us without question			
(a) wives to husbands	77	65	10
(b) citizens to governments	73	55	10
It is the devil who plants doubt and uncertainty in peoples' minds	100	90	33
	n = 30	n = 20	n = 30

NCC = New church charistmatics
ECC = Established church charismatics
MCT = Mainline church traditionalists

New church charismatics were virtually unanimous in their conservative fundamentalism on all of the items in Table 18. Their particularism and ethnocentrism is evident in the belief that eternal life is only for born-again Christians and that a practising religious Hindu could not gain eternal life.

The established church charismatic respondents were almost unanimous in their belief in the literal truth of the Bible and belief in hell, the devil, and his presence when there is doubt and uncertainty in peoples' minds. They differed from the new church charismatic respondents on the chances of salvation of non born-again Christians but their chances remain slim. The established church charismatic sample was also much less unanimous than the new church charismatic sample about submission to governments. The mainline church trad- itional group was not fundamentalist on any of the items. In terms of the literal truth of the Bible, the Satanic origin of doubt and uncertainty, and submission to husbands and governments, they appear to be anti-fundamentalist.

Kelley's (1977) contention that absolutism is a consequence of total commitment is supported by responses to the statement: "I am not sure that I have found the meaning and purpose of life".

Percentage responses for each sample group were as follows:

	Agree	Uncertain	Disagree
	%	%	%
New church charismatics	0	0	100
Established church charismatics	5	0	95
Mainline church traditionalists	30	23	47

More than half the mainline church traditional respondents were not sure that they had found the meaning and purpose of life whereas the new church charismatic and established church charismatic respondents were unanimous in the certainty that they had found it. We can conclude then that Charismatic churches in general are succeeding in providing their members with a clear explanation of the meaning of life whereas traditional mainline churches are not.

8.7.2 Suffering

The new churches teach that all suffering: illness, psychological problems and poverty, is Satanic in origin. To test how respondents understood suffering they were asked the following question: "One sees

innocent people suffering every day. What does this mean?" and
given four alternatives to choose from. (See Table 19 below.)

TABLE 19: UNDERSTANDING OF SUFFERING

Percentage of respondents in each sample group who explained
suffering in the following ways:

	NCC %	ECC %	MCT %
It is part of God's plan	0	30	14
It is the work of the devil	80	10	7
It sometimes makes me wonder whether there is a God	0	0	7
I don't understand - God does not want people to suffer	20	60	72

If answered: It is the work of the devil:

Percentage respondents in each sample group who specifically
agreed that the devil caused the following:

	NCC %	ECC %	MCT %
Psychological problems	77	10	7
Illness	77	5	3
Poverty	73	5	3
	n = 30	n = 20	n = 30

NCC = New church charismatics
ECC = Established church charismatics
MCT = Mainline church traditionalists

The vast majority of new church charismatics saw suffering as the work
of the devil, whereas most mainline church traditionalists said they
did not understand its causes although they were sure that God
did not want people to suffer. A significant percentage of established
church charismatics thought that suffering was part of God's plan
but the majority said that they did not understand why innocent
people suffered.

The very different understanding which the new church charismatic group

has of suffering is relevant on two counts: firstly they <u>have</u> an
explanation whereas most mainline church members do not, secondly
the nature of the explanation is completely 'spiritual' (i.e. non-
secular) which must have an effect on the kind of action used to
combat it. If respondents said that suffering was the work of
the devil they were asked whether the devil was responsible for
the following: physical illness, poverty and psychological problems.
Over 90 percent of the new church charismatics who said that the
devil caused suffering agreed that he was responsible for the
specific forms of suffering mentioned.

The hypothesis that new churches appeal during times of insecurity
because of the absolute answers they provide is supported by the
fact that the new church charismatic group was the only group which
had an absolute explanation for suffering. The nature of the explanation is also significant. If all suffering is caused by the
devil, then by implication only people who allow the devil into
their lives will suffer. Christian responsibility regarding the
suffering of others then only extends to spreading the gospel.

This attitude was confirmed by the following comments regarding
illness:

- *I realised I was sick because I was a sinner.*
- *Sickness and psychological problems are because of
  the devil - he attacks us in the way that we can't
  handle.*
- *I realised one doesn't have to be sick and accept one's
  fate as the Dutch Reformed Church teaches.*

8.7.3 Prosperity and poverty

The new churches teach that prosperity is God's will and poverty is
Satan's domain. The solution provided by the new churches to financial
difficulties is simple and absolute: work your finances according to
God's laws and you will not be poor. The implication for attitudes
towards the poor and poverty in general is obvious. Respondents were

asked to agree or disagree with certain statements designed to assess
their attitudes towards prosperity and poverty. (See Table 20 below).

TABLE 20: ATTITUDES TOWARDS PROSPERITY AND POVERTY

Percentage of respondents in each sample group who agreed with the
following statements:

	NCC %	ECC %	MCT %
God wants us to be financially prosperous	86	45	21
There is nothing bad or ungodly about being financially prosperous	97	90	80
We should be generous in giving because he who casts his bread upon the waters shall have it returned ten-fold	80	65	57
Poverty is mainly caused by weakness and lack of faith	43	30	7
	n = 30	n = 20	n = 30

NCC = New church charismatics
ECC = Established church charismatics
MCT = Mainline church traditionalists

Table 20 reveals that while the vast majority of all respondents agreed
that there was nothing bad or ungodly about being financially prosperous,
there was a large discrepancy between groups concerning God's active
desire for people to be financially prosperous. Eighty six percent of
new church charismatic respondents agreed that this was so, compared
with 45 percent of established church charismatic respondents and only
21 percent of mainline church traditional respondents. The statement
concerning giving was made to establish respondents' motives for giving
rather than their agreement with the principle. Significantly more
new church charismatic respondents than established church respondents
agreed that the motive for giving was to get back. New church charismatic
respondents thus accept this part of the prosperity message.

Interviews with new church charismatic respondents confirmed that the
prosperity teachings and implications thereof are accepted and practised

by new church charismatic members:

- *The faith teachings explained what had always bugged me. I learnt that as a Christian I didn't have to be poverty-stricken. I was motivated to be successful and had felt uncomfortable.*

- *I learnt that the Lord wanted us to be successful. You can be a Christian and be successful at the same time.*

- *You've got to prosper spiritually first - lots of people expect financial prosperity first.*

- *Let Jesus mind your business - he's your senior Jewish partner.*

- *We have prospered materially but we're still waiting for the big one. He'll make good his promise.*

- *I left my job because God told me to. We had always lived highly and suddenly it was the last meal. I was beginning to enjoy putting my God to the test - 2 hours later someone slid R20 under the door. Three hours later under the windscreen was a cheque.*

- *We have rules for prosperity - if you don't tithe the devourer will come.*

Pastors interviewed were asked to explain the prosperity message and their reactions to criticisms of it. Their explanation of prosperity did not in any way contradict the description of it in Chapter 3.1. The response to criticisms of it was that these were based on an imperfect understanding of the Bible and what God's promises are for people.

The corollary to the prosperity message is that poverty is a sign of being out of line with God's will. People are poor because they are not working according to God's laws. If they are not working according to these laws they are in the devil's domain and are oppressed by him. We have seen that most new church charismatics (80%) regard suffering as being the work of the devil and of these the vast majority view poverty specifically as being caused by Satan.

To further test whether new church charismatic respondents regarded poverty as being the fault of the individuals concerned they were asked to agree or disagree with the statement: "Poverty is mainly caused by weakness and lack of faith". Disagreement was taken to

indicate a more secular understanding of the reasons for poverty.
Fifty percent of the new church charismatics, 70 percent of the
established church charismatics and 90 percent of the mainline church
traditionalists disagreed with this statement, confirming the suggestion that new church charismatics tend to explain poverty in non-
secular ways.

The pastors were generally more outspoken about poverty than the
respondents. All of them said that poverty was caused by Satan and
most said that the reason why there was poverty in the third world
was because the gospel had not been heard there. The following responses typify their explanations of poverty:

- *In countries where the gospel is proclaimed (e.g. South
  Africa, United States of America) they have the blessing
  of God.*

- *India is rife with demons - you can sense the presence
  of evil there - that's why they are so poor and there
  is so much suffering there.*

Spontaneous comments from new church charismatic respondents revealed
that new church members accept the teachings of their pastors
regarding poverty:

- *Poverty - of course this is his domain - if you're not
  serving God you're serving the devil.*
- *Nations that are ungodly don't prosper.*
- *There's an evil spirit of poverty.*
- *There is a curse on Africans in this country because of
  their witchcraft.*

When asked how they explained that Christians could be poor (e.g. black
South African Christians) the pastors either said that they were not
born-again Christians or that they had not learnt how to operate in the
laws of God.

Pastors were asked whether the prosperity message applied absolutely to
anyone regardless of race or class. All agreed that this was the case.

A scenario was then painted of a poor black man and a rich white man of the same age being 'saved' and beginning to operate God's laws for prosperity. Pastors were asked whether these two men had the same chance to achieve prosperity. The fatal flaw in the prosperity message is perhaps best exemplified by the following examples of responses to this question:

- *Well it's a relative thing depending on where you live.*
- *Individual needs are not the same.*
- *In Malawi you're a rich man if you own a bicycle.*
- *How can you believe God for a BMW when you only earn R60 a month.*
- *My garden boy is prospering. He's born-again and I pay him a good salary.*
- *People in Umbilo find an abundant life that is not satisfying to someone in Kloof.*

In addition to teaching that prosperity is scriptural, at least one new church, the Durban Christian Centre, does not leave this to chance but helps its members to achieve prosperity in more practical ways. It runs an unemployment ministry, helping unemployed people to find jobs once they have been taught the promises and conditions of prosperity. The Durban Christian Centre's (DCC) unemployment ministry lecture notes state: "Emphasise that the evil one has come to give sin, sickness and poverty".

An additional service provided by the Durban Christian Centre is to advise ailing businesses on how to run on scriptural lines. This consists of initially looking at the Managing Director's personal life - his relationships with God, the government, his wife and children and the body, and who he delegates authority to. "First of all we pray for those in authority, then we start encouraging them to get into knowledge of the Word." The next step is to define the vision which the Managing Director has for that company. Through prayer and obedience to God's Word the vision then becomes a reality, according to the head of Durban Christian Centre's financial ministry who was himself an extremely successful businessman.

Certain businesses tithe 10 percent of their incomes to the new churches.
The magazines and newspapers put out by the new churches contain advertisements for shops and businesses 'dedicated to the Lord'.   Traditional
Christianity's reluctance to discuss secular capitalist interests along with
spiritual concerns is not a feature of the new churches.

8.7.4 The social gospel

New church pastors were asked whether the church had any part to play
in improving social conditions.   They all agreed that it did have a
part to play but that it had nothing to do with 'politics'.   The
churches' duty socially was to get the gospel out and to teach people
'how to lay hold of God's blessings'.   It was clearly stated by
pastors that once spiritual problems were taken care of, the social
problems would take care of themselves.   All of the pastors
criticised the social gospel as being either wishy washy/political/
a social work program.   The following statements from pastors reflect
the attitude towards the social gospel:

> - *The mainline churches are just covering everything*
>   *with love and sympathy.*
> - *Christians should start praying for change ......*
>   *instead of fawning all over the blacks.*

The new church pastors interviewed were adamant that the church should
not involve itself with politics and that the duty of the church and
Christians was only and simply to pray - for the government and for
the country.   In support of the non-involvement of the church
and Christians with political issues the pastors quoted Romans 13:1&2.
Rebellion, they said, was a Satanic principle which led only to chaos
which was also Satanic.

Table 21 results (below) indicate that new church charismatic respondents
support and adhere to the teachings of their pastors.

TABLE 21: PERCEPTION OF SOUTH AFRICA'S PROBLEMS

Percentage of respondents in each sample group who made the
following spontaneous statements about South Africa:

	NCC	ECC	MCT
	%*	%*	%*
Prayer is the only solution	72	35	6
God has placed the government here	32	6	6
God is for apartheid	16	0	0
Things are changing/the spirit of God is working in South Africa	56	18	0
We don't want chaos/ this is the only way the country can run	16	29	13
Rebellion and chaos are from Satan	16	0	0
Negative statements about the government	8	41	88
	n = 30	n = 20	n = 30

NCC = New church charismatics
ECC = Established church charismatics
MCT = Mainline church traditionalists
* Respondents could give more than one response

We have already seen that the vast majority of new church charismatic
respondents believed in submission without question to governments
(see Table 18, p.101).   Although the majority of all three sample
groups agreed that "The only way this country will come right is
through prayer and the spreading of the gospel", (see Table 9, p.77)
the differences between them become clearer when open-ended responses
about political attitudes are examined.

While 72 percent of new church charismatic respondents spontaneously
said that prayer was the only solution to this country's problems,
only 35 percent of established church charismatic respondents and 6
percent of mainline church traditional respondents spontaneously said
this.   After prayer, the most common statements concerning political
change by new church charismatic respondents concerned the belief
that the spirit of God was working things out and that things were
changing.

Basically the belief of new church charismatic respondents seemed to be that God was in charge, that he had placed the government here, that the spirit of God was moving and changing things and that the duties of a Christian were to pray and intercede for the government. The following responses typify this attitude:

- *God has put a law in this land: you don't go against it no matter what you think individually.*

- *Governments are God-appointed even Mao. Christianity grew in China because Mao had made one official language.*

- *God has put all governments here.*

- *They are there because God allows them to be.*

- *The government is scriptural - there are people there to serve.*

- *Now I vote Nationalist - it is best for the circumstances especially with their God-fearing/loving background.*

- *Before I was heavy into politics - a PFP fanatic, then I became a liberal Nationalist. When I was born-again I lost interest in politics because I was more interested in the affairs of God.*

- *Rebellion is a Satanic principle - to rebel is going against God. If you pray for the government the nation prospers and there's peace in the world. By praying one is not being passive - actually it's a spiritual warfare.*

- *If God doesn't want them he'll remove them.*

- *Why are we trying to do what God and Jesus couldn't do?*

- *Politics is not your business it's God's business.*

- *The spirit of the Lord is moving for racial harmony.*

- *If the blacks think they're hard done by you should have seen the Romans.*

- *If God doesn't want them he'll remove them. I don't get involved because I know God is in control - I leave it to God's hands - I pray that he will open the eyes of the leaders and guide them.*

- *If God wanted it otherwise He would do it.*

- *I can't see any link between loving your neighbour and getting involved in politics.*

- *If Jesus came to South Africa He would not look at the political structure - discrimination is a minor thing.*

- *I'm not interested in politics and haven't really thought about the future. I'm just positive about it - the Lord will work things out.*

- *You'd like to change things but the law says you can't so you can't.   Maybe it is unjust but so what.*
- *Now I vote Nat. because of their God-fearing background.*

There appears to be a strong evangelical desire and a belief in divine intervention amongst many respondents in the sample.   Either this indicates a powerful faith in God or a powerful desire to avoid active participation in social change.   However, charismatics are much more unanimous in their belief in prayer and evangelism as the only solution to this country's problems.   This raises the question as to whether a commitment to Charismatic Christianity somehow encourages lack of engagement in social action.

New church charismatics evidence the greatest tendency to pray and spread the gospel in preference to any other kind of social intervention.   Taken in conjunction with their strong conviction that the church has nothing to do with social change (see Table 15, p.94) and their strong political conservatism and attitudes towards suffering, it appears that the new churches are well suited to their needs.

8.8 RECRUITMENT TO THE NEW CHURCHES

New church charismatic respondents were asked how they had come to know about the Christian Centre. Results were as follows:

TABLE 22: RECRUITMENT CHANNELS

Percentage of new church charismatic respondents who joined the Christian Centre via the following:

	%
Friends	47
Following a pastor	30
Family	13
Chance/media	10

More than half the sample (60%) had heard about the Christian Centre through friends or family. A significant percentage (30%) of respondents had followed a pastor when he had left an established church, or had gone to the Christian Centre because the particular pastor was there. Only 10 percent of the new church charismatic sample had heard about the Christian Centre by chance: walking past, media campaigns, chance evangelising, etc. The new churches in Durban do not however rely on recruitment via pre-existing social networks. They advertise themselves on a much larger scale than the established churches, evidenced by their large prominent advertisements in newspapers and more recently the distribution by the Durban Christian Centre of a free newspaper, Christian New Testament Times.

Our findings, however, support the previously mentioned hypothesis that recruitment is largely via pre-existing social networks. They also suggest that the personality of the pastor is an important factor in choosing or staying in the new churches.

8.8.1 Church attendance histories

Table 6 (p. 70) reveals that the majority of new church charismatic
respondents (76%) had changed denominations twice or more than twice.
Taken in conjunction with the fact that many (43%) had been saved
in Pentecostal churches or evangelical campaigns (see Table 24) a
picture begins to emerge of the new churches as being either the
final resting place after a long search or perhaps only yet another
stepping stone in the search for a spiritual home.

Table 23 shows that Pentecostal churches are the single most common
source of membership of the new churches, followed by the Methodist
church with a significantly smaller percentage coming from Anglican,
Roman Catholic and Presbyterian, Lutheran, Dutch Reformed Church
and other non-conformist churches.

TABLE 23: IMMEDIATE PAST CHURCH

Percentage of respondents in each sample group whose previous
denomination was:

	NCC %	ECC %	MCT %
Roman Catholic	7	0	8
Anglican	10	13	25
Methodist	23	33	25
Presbyterian	3	0	0
Pentecostal	30	13	0
Other (Dutch Reformed, Christian Scientist, non-conformist, fringe)	27	33	33
	n = 30	n = 20	n = 30

NCC = New church charismatics
ECC = Established church charismatics
MCT = Mainline church traditionalists

8.9 CONVERSION

Charismatic respondents were asked where they had been born-again/
saved (see Table 24 below):

TABLE 24:   SETTING FOR ORIGINAL SALVATIONAL EXPERIENCE

Percentage respondents in the charismatic samples who had undergone
original salvational experience in the following settings:

	NCC	ECC
	%	%
Christian Centre	30	5
Pentecostal churches	24	20
Evangelical campaigns	20	15
Mainline churches	10	45
Other - small group/alone	16	15
	n = 30	n = 20

NCC = New church charismatics
ECC = Established church charismatics

The results support the general hypothesis that the conversion
experience mainly occurs in a group setting.   Seventy percent
of the new church charismatic sample had experienced their
conversions outside of the Christian Centre.   This is partly
explained by the fact that a significant proportion of the new
church charismatic sample (40%) had been saved for more than 5
years (i.e. longer than the Christian Centre's existence).   (See
Table 52, p.192).   It does, however, seem to suggest that a
significant proportion of the new church charismatics are joining
the new churches once they are already born-again perhaps because
they feel that the new churches are most suited to their needs as
charismatics.

A significant proportion of the new churches sample had been converted in Pentecostal churches (24%).   In conjunction with the results in Table 23 (Immediate Past Church), which indicate that Pentecostal churches are the most common source of membership of the new churches, the implication seems to be that the new churches are somehow catering better for charismatic needs than other charismatic churches.

Only 10 percent of the new church charismatic sample had been born-again in mainline churches although 43 percent (see Table 23) were ex mainline church members.   The largest proportion of the new church charismatic sample thus came from mainline churches, a fact which must be of some concern to the leaders of the mainline churches.

As far as the established church charismatic sample was concerned, the majority (65%) had experienced conversion in either Pentecostal or mainline churches.   In conjunction with the fact that the majority of the established church charismatic sample (75%) had only changed churches once or never changed churches, and in conjunction with the fact that the majority (65%) of the established church charismatic sample said they were completely satisfied with their church (see Table 34, p. 145) the implication appears to be that certain charismatics are being satisfied by the established churches.

8.10 FORM AND STYLE OF SERVICES

The services at the Christian Centre follow a relatively consistent
pattern.   The service begins with the singing of many gospel hymns
accompanied by a band and gospel singers on the stage.   Early on
in the service people are welcomed and asked to greet people around
them.   Announcements are made concerning coming meetings, seminars,
home fellowships, etc.   A prayer follows which usually contains a
plea that those in authority may be given wisdom and guidance.   In
addition people in the army are prayed for.

Participation by people at the service is elicited by asking people
questions to which answers are called or hands raised.   Examples
heard were:

- *Is the Holy Spirit welcome here today?*
- *How many of you were saved in the last year?*
- *How many of you are here for the first time?*
- *How many of you are visitors to Durban?*
- *How many of you have attended our Spiritual Growth Seminars?*

Throughout the service songs are sung with hands raised or hand-
clapping and there is regular changing from sitting down to standing
up according to the directives of the pastor.

The main speaker, who has usually not participated up to this point,
then takes over and begins his sermon.   The following were the most
common themes heard by observers attending the services:

- Christians knowing who they are in Christ
- the power and courage displayed by certain characters
  in the Bible
- the prosperity which certain characters in the Bible
  enjoyed
- the benefits of the Holy Spirit
- the revival that South Africa is experiencing
- the end times.

Sermons are delivered in a very personal Americanised style.
Pastors refer to their own experiences, visions and messages with
phrases like *"The Lord has laid it upon my heart to ......"*, *"The
Lord showed me...."*, The impression is distinctly created that
the speaker has direct contact with God or revelation from God.

An unexpected feature of the observed services was direct reference
to, comparison with and criticism of the mainline churches, which
generally elicited laughter from the congregation.   Examples of
this are:

- *We believe in water baptism we don't believe in dry-cleaning*
  (referring to christening).
- *You can't be educated into salvation* (referring to
  confirmation classes).
- *The dead can't praise God* (referring to traditional
  church services and hymns).

At a certain point in the services, offerings are called for.
People are generally instructed to let the Holy Spirit minister
to them and guide them in how much to give.   (*"Give until it hurts"* -
Ray McCauley.)

The climax of the meeting is the altar call which follows the sermon.
While the gospel singers sing quietly in the background, the pastor
appeals to people who have not yet taken Jesus into their lives but
who now want to do this to raise their hands.   He may refer to
the emptiness or loneliness that cannot be filled by anyone except
Jesus.   The atmosphere is intense and emotional.   Once people
have raised their hands the pastor urges them to step into the
aisles and come forward.   Once they are standing at the altar
they recite a confession after the pastor - The Sinner's Prayer.

The saved people are then told that they are saved.   A team of
counsellors steps forward and the new converts are taken out of
the auditorium to be individually counselled and told about the
infilling of the Holy Spirit, water baptism and courses which they
should attend at the Bible College.   Personal details are recorded
and converts are 'followed-up'.

After the altar call comes the healing line. This takes different
forms: sometimes people are healed in their seats and told to
come forward only if they have already been healed, sometimes
specific complaints are called for, for example anybody who
has asthma or a sore shoulder. Once people are lined up in
front of the stage the annointed healer lays hands on each person
individually, rebuking the illness and commanding it to leave in
the name of Jesus. At this point many people fall over backwards
and are caught by catchers and laid on the floor. This
experience is referred to as being slain in the spirit.

If one analyses these services in terms of Glock and Stark's
(1973) and Argyle's (1975) conversion models the following
similarities emerge:

Emotional appeals: from the outset the services are emotional
and exuberant. People hug each other, clap and raise their hands
and there is a high level of participation by the congregation in
terms of singing, responding to questions and shouting "amen" and
"hallelujah". The people who are already saved look happy and
confident and totally absorbed in the proceedings. The display-
ing of emotion is clearly permissible and obviously desirable.
There is a sense as an unsaved observer of being bombarded with
stimuli. No single activity is continued for very long with
people constantly being instructed to sit, stand, raise hands,
clap hands, respond verbally, sing, etc.

Although there are no hellfire and brimstone appeals to raise
anxiety, there are many references to the end times and the
security only obtained by "knowing who one is in Christ."

- *The end time is coming. Don't think things are going to get better in the world - they're going to get worse.*

- *Everywhere there's trouble.....*

- *I believe that World War 3 is coming....*

- *Later will be Armageddon where Jesus comes with us and destroys the armies of the anti-Christ.*

- *I believe there will be war by 1985.*

- *I don't want to frighten you because you know who you are in Christ.*

- *God is preparing us to go into the battle and gain the victory.*

The speakers, whether they are from overseas or not, appear to have a particular style of delivery reminiscent of a deep South Baptist preacher. American accents and phrases are common regardless of the origin of the pastors.

Throughout the services there are signs and wonders - proof that what is being claimed is true. People cry, speak in tongues, are slain in the spirit, saved and healed. The pastors deliver testimonies about healings, they tell the congregation how many people were saved, about how many people are leaving the Dutch Reformed church, about how the Lord is working mightily and about visions and prophecies. The implication is constantly that something powerful is happening.

Thus group pressure, public commitment, the characteristics of the speaker and personal influence (of counsellors) facilitate and encourage conversion.

8.11 RELIGIOUS EXPERIENCE

In accordance with their charismatic origins the new churches insist
on a definitive salvational experience. At some definite time a
person is saved and makes a confession of faith declaring that he/she
accepts Christ as saviour and Lord. Many respondents reported the
extreme emotion felt when they were saved or born-again:

- *I felt called to go up at Living Waters - I didn't want to I
  was crying and shaking - then I confessed and felt so relieved.*

- *I didn't want to go up. There was an altar call. I was
  just sitting there crying. The pastor came into the pews and
  begged people to come for salvation - I went up and accepted
  the Lord.*

- *There was an altar call. I said I would give my life to the
  Lord if he took my habit* (smoking) *away. After church I
  sobbed my heart out and gave my life to the Lord.*

- *They had an altar call and I couldn't stop crying. My hand
  just shot out of its socket and I was slain in the spirit -
  500 witnessed it.*

- *When I was saved it felt as if heat was running through my
  head and body. It felt like rain falling on my head -
  like water - oil - living water.*

It must be noted however, that the majority of the new church charismatic
sample were not 'saved' at the Christian Centre, but in other settings.

After the initial salvational experience new church members are
required to receive the baptism of the Holy Spirit. According to
the pastors and members of the new churches speaking in tongues is
a necessary and compulsory sign of being "infilled" with the Holy
Spirit. Although pastors indicated that other gifts (charisms) of
the Holy Spirit were equally important, it is clear from their
terminology (it is referred to as the baptism of the Holy Spirit)
and from the significance attributed to the experience by respondents,
that speaking in tongues is central to their experience.

- *I went up to receive the Holy Spirit and started shaking.
  My knees were knocking and I thought, 'Is this cold or
  what?'   Tears were streaming.   I said, 'God give it to me'.
  This woman said 'you've got it' - the words - the words kept
  coming - it's just too beautiful, wonderful.   I just kept
  shouting - 'I did it, I did it'.   I left with one word,
  shaking and after that added one word at a time.*

- *I prayed for tongues audibly - as I opened my mouth to ask
  again my mouth started shaking and my tongue started shooting
  in my mouth - I felt enveloped in love and could see Jesus
  standing right there - it babbled right out.*

Another common experience reported by the new church charismatic
sample was 'being slain in the spirit'.   This consists of as one
respondent put it *'being unable to stand from the force of God's
power'.*

It was clear from discussions with the new church charismatic
respondents that being slain in the spirit is a valued and significant
experience.   Many of the respondents reported that they had initially
been resistant to the idea, believing it to be exaggerated or
unnecessary, but that they had been forced to revise their opinions
after they themselves had experienced being slain:

- *I was slain in the spirit and I·was trembling and couldn't
  control myself.   The pastor blew on me and I hit the
  ground again.*

- *You collapse - it's the power of the Holy Spirit falling
  on you.   The sensation inside you is joyful - your knees
  cave in.*

- *I went up to the front for healing and was slain before I
  got there - it was so heavy - I've never felt such power
  in my life - like electricity.*

- *I was slain in the spirit recently - I could feel my whole
  body going warm and I fainted.*

- *You are just pinned to the ground - drunk in the spirit.*

- *A lot needn't fall.   I'm one of those who don't fall unless
  I have to.*

- *My body just relaxed and I couldn't hold myself up - I was
  filled with joy and started praising Him.*

- *The first time I was prayed for I took a deep breath and was slain in the spirit - I used to think it was hypnosis but I was down on the floor - it's a beautiful feeling - I didn't want to stop it.*

- *The pastor prayed for me and down I went - bam.*

- *You cannot stand up under the power of God. I was sceptical but it came at me like a wall and pushed me backwards.*

- *I asked God to give me the Holy Spirit and I felt the power - it's like electricity running through your body. You feel weak and want to fall over. I resisted this and stopped myself from falling to the ground - I have since learnt at the Durban Christian Centre not to resist but to let the Holy Spirit work through you.*

Another experience which was commonly described by charismatic respondents was that of experiencing the power of the Holy Spirit. This is not as dramatic as being slain in the spirit and was described in the following ways by respondents:

- *You feel that power in you - you just start shaking with the power of God in you - your body gets used to it.*

- *I have felt the Spirit of God on me - it's like electricity through you - you start shaking.*

- *It's like rivers of living waters.*

- *Sometimes you tingle it's just beautiful - He's there.*

- *I could feel like a river of warmth going round my body like a life-giving force - continual emotion - through my body - electrifying.*

- *soft rain.*

- *When the Holy Spirit comes on you it feels as if you are wallowing in the Dead Sea - it's a delicious ray of safety and comfort - it washes over you as if it has complete control over you.*

Respondents were asked whether the presence of God had ever physically affected them. Percentage positive responses were as follows for each sample group:

	%
new church charismatics	100
established church charismatics	90
mainline church traditionals	17

Respondents were then asked to describe two of the most dramatic examples of being physically affected by God's presence.

TABLE 25: RELIGIOUS EXPERIENCE

Percentage of respondents in each sample group who experienced God's presence in the following ways:

	NCC %*	ECC %*	MCT %*
Baptism of the Holy Spirit (speaking in tongues)	67	65	16
Power of the Holy Spirit	53	53	16
Slain in the spirit	43	18	0
Visions	17	12	0
Other	0	5	67
	n = 30	n = 20	n = 30

* Respondents could give more than one response

NCC = New church charismatics
ECC = Established church charismatics
MCT = Mainline church traditionalists

It is clear from the above table that speaking in tongues is the most common and dramatic kind of religious experience which charismatics have. Experiencing the power of the Holy Spirit is important for all charismatics. Comparing the new church charismatics and the established church charismatic's frequency of being slain in the spirit, it can be inferred that this is a particularly new church, as opposed to a generally charismatic phenomenon.

The high percentage of mainline church traditional responses in the 'Other' category is explained by the fact that most of the mainline church traditional respondents' experiences were undramatic and consisted of the following kinds of responses.

- *I have felt very close to God.*

- *Tremendous peace came over me when I had the operation.*

- *I had a fantastic feeling at a service but I can get the same feeling when I run - exhilaration.*

The fact that only 17 percent of mainline church traditional respondents had experienced God's physical presence, compared with the dramatic nature of the religious experiences of new church chraismatic respondents (all of whom had had such experiences) for example:

- *I prayed and the Lord audibly said, "I will help you" - then I heard a great and mighty wind and couldn't turn over because of the wind coming through the window (but it was a still night).*

points to a clear distinction between charismatics and non-charismatics.

8.11.1 Miracles

Miracles can be taken to be another manifestation of God's tangible power. Respondents were asked whether God had ever performed a miracle in their lives. Percentage affirmative responses were as follows for each sample group:

	%
new church charismatics	100
established church charismatics	90
mainline church traditionals	37

Only 37 percent of the mainline church traditionals feel that God has performed a miracle in their lives compared with the vast majority of charismatics (100% of new church charismatics, 90% of established church charismatics). The kinds of miracles which were described by

respondents when asked to give some of the most outstanding examples
are indicative of the expectations of the different groups.   (See
Table 26 below.)

TABLE 26: MIRACLES

Percentage respondents in each sample group who had experienced the
following kinds of miracles:

	NCC %*	ECC %*	MCT %*
Personal healing	**47	**40	5
Material gain	**43	**15	5
General blessing	**30	**25	**35
Healing by respondent	**30	15	0
Salvation of respondent	**27	**25	5
Healing of loved one	23	5	**10
Occupational improvement	20	10	5
Intervention by God - changing weather, providing accommodation	17	15	**10
Inner healing (emotional)	13	10	5
Being saved from death	13	5	**15
Salvation of loved one	10	**25	0
Improvement in relationship	7	5	**50
Giving up smoking	7	10	0
Visions	7	10	0
	n = 30	n = 20	n = 30

  * Respondents could give more than one response
 ** Indicates 5 most common kinds of miracle for each group

NCC = New church charismatics
ECC = Established church charismatics
MCT = Mainline church traditionalists

Apart from general blessing, which was a common miracle for all groups,
the mainline church traditional group differed significantly from the
new church charismatic and established church charismatic groups who
commonly named the same kinds of miracles.

For the mainline church traditionalist respondents the most outstanding miracle was a good marriage, good children and/or improvement in marriage and children.   This is possibly indicative of learnt expectations as to what can reasonably be expected from God.   In mainline church traditionalist terms, God can bless a person's life generally, but there appears little expectation on the part of the mainline church traditionalists that God can or does powerfully or actively intervene in their lives.

The following were typical responses from mainline church traditionalist respondents:

- *God has helped me in general.*

- *My husband - the way my marriage has developed.*

- *God showed me my wife.*

- *I have had a tremendous number of blessings and assistance.*

- *Each of my children.*

- *I was unemployed, prayed for a door to be opened.*

The new church charismatics and established church charismatics on the contrary, saw God as performing very definite and dramatic miracles in their lives.   Personal healing of respondents was the most common miracle for both established church charismatics and new church charismatics, but a significantly greater percentage of new church charismatics said that they personally had healed someone.   (This supports the hypothesis that the feeling of power attained by new church charismatics is an important element in the appeal of the new churches.)

The high percentage of new church charismatics who named material gain as a miracle in their lives is predictable from their belief in the prosperity message.   The following were typical miracles described by new church charismatic respondents:

- *This house for a start - how God provides when you live according to his law. We knew it was God's house for us. It cost R18 000, now we're selling it for R95 000 - it's all part of God's plan.*

- *He prayed and my leg just went zoop.*

- *We cursed the growth in Jesus' mighty name.*

- *The Lord took my smoking away just like that.*

- *I couldn't pay my rent and prayed and a postal order arrived in the post.*

- *I was moved to give money so gave my whole bonus. The next day my boss phoned to say I had an increase.*

- *R300 was put in my pocket just when I had a large bank overdraft.*

- *We wanted cool weather and the weather report said there would be a heat wave. We laughed and said 'Devil you're a liar'. We prayed and said 'Wind blow in Jesus' name' - it rained.*

8.12   CHANGES IN PERSONAL AND SOCIAL LIFE

Conversion indicates a change in the individual's perception of himself/herself and of the world. Full religious commitment is seen as a total response to a total demand (Kelley, 1977).   Therefore we hypothesised that conversion, in the sense of being born-again, and membership of charismatic churches would bring about a dramatic change in the individuals' personal and social lives.

8.12.1 Changes in personal life

Respondents were asked how they felt about themselves now compared with how they felt about themselves before they were born-again/ five years previously.   (See Table 27 below.)

TABLE 27: CHANGES IN PERSONAL LIFE			
Percentage respondents in each sample group whose lives had changed in the following ways:	NCC	ECC	MCT
	%*	%*	%*
More confident; more secure; before lacked confidence	**53	**35	**23
Have power; victorious, in control	**30	0	0
Less anxious/fearful	**30	**25	7
Before selfish, critical, resentful	**27	0	0
Now peaceful/contented, relaxed	**27	**25	10
Now have direction and purpose	23	20	7
More loving, compassionate, trusting, patient	23	**30	**30
Cope better through God	23	**35	**17
Like self better/better understanding of self	20	5	7
Total change	20	20	3
Now happy, joyful, enthusiastic, positive	20	5	10
Have no worries; have handed over	17	5	3
Before worried about future, not now	17	20	3
More mature/responsible/general growth	10	**25	**30
Before felt worthless, just existing	7	0	0
Growth in faith	0	**30	**27
Cope better through age, maturity	0	0	**17
Negative change	0	0	3
No change	0	0	**17
	n = 30	n = 20	n = 30
* Respondents could give more than one response			
** Indicates 5 most frequent kinds of changes for each group			
NCC = New church charismatics ECC = Established church charismatics MCT = Mainline church traditionalists			

Results show that all groups commonly stated that they were more confident or secure at present, or that they had previously lacked confidence. However a significantly higher percentage of new church charismatic respondents said that they were more confident, which supports the power deprivation theory discussed previously. The fact that the new church charismatic group were the only group who said that they now had power and were victorious, and that this was the second most frequent kind of personal change for this group, provides further strong support for the power deprivation theory.

Typical responses from new church charismatic respondents in this area were:

- *I'm much more confident - nothing is impossible.*

- *Life is worth living for - before I didn't feel worth anything.*

- *Life has purpose and meaning and I'm able to face the future with confidence.*

A common change for both the new church charismatic and established church charismatic groups was that they were now less anxious and fearful than they had been. When combined with the stated change of before having been worried or fearful about the future but now not worrying, a clear picture emerges for the three groups:

	NCC %	ECC %	MCT %
Less anxious, fearful generally/about the future	47	45	10

Significantly more new church charismatic respondents than established church charismatic respondents specifically stated that they now had no worries.

- *I have no worries now. I'm totally committed: everything is handed over to Him for example the sale of this house is all His move.*

Even if people who are attracted to charismatic Christianity were more fearful than average to begin with, there is clearly something about charismatic Christianity which is allaying people's fears.

A significant difference was found between the new church charismatics and the rest of the sample on self-criticism of past behaviour. Twenty-seven percent of the new church charismatic group stated that they had previously been selfish, bitter, critical or resentful while none of the rest of the sample said this. This may be a result of the emphasis in the new churches on giving testimonies which depend upon a dramatic improvement in behaviour.

Changes which differentiated the new church charismatic group from the rest of the sample were:
- Now better liking or understanding of self.
- Now happy joyful, enthusiastic, positive.
- Now have no worries, have handed over.

Changes which differentiated charismatics generally from the mainline traditional group were:
- Now have direction and purpose.
- Total change.

The fact that charismatics feel that they now have direction and purpose in life supports Kelley's (1977) need for meaning hypothesis. Significantly more charismatics said that they felt totally different about themselves now. This supports the contention that part of the strength of a conservative church is that it demands and expects a total change in lifestyle and self- perception.

The established church respondents experienced more changes than the new church charismatic group in the following ways:
- More loving, compassionate, trusting, patient.
- More mature, responsible.
- Stronger faith.

These changes are likely to be attributable to age and general maturity and need not have anything to do with the influence of the church.

8.12.2 Changes in social life

Respondents were asked whether their social life had changed since they had been born-again or/in the last 5 years.

    83 percent of new church charismatics said their social life had changed completely

    35 percent of established church charismatics said their social life had changed completely

     0 percent of mainline church traditionalists said their social life had changed completely.

When asked how their social lives had changed (see Table 28 below) the new church charismatic respondents were generally insistent that there had been no constraints placed on them to change their behaviour but that they personally had wanted to change their behaviour, friends and social activities.

The following comments from various new church charismatic respondents were very typical:

    - *You don't have time for anything else if you're committed.*

    - *You feel like a new creation. I have a demanding job - the Lord takes up the rest of my time.*

TABLE 28: CHANGES IN SOCIAL LIFE

Percentage of respondents in each sample group whose social lives had changed in the following ways:

	NCC %	ECC %	MCT %
Complete change	83	35	0
Somewhat changed	14	30	20
No change	3	35	80

Percentage of respondents in each sample group who said that their social lives had changed in the following ways:	NCC %*	ECC %*	MCT %*
Used to drink - no longer drink	50	35	6
Used to dance and go to parties - no longer	50	29	6
Now socialise mainly with born-again Christians/ committed Christians	47	41	12
Now do mainly Christian things	33	29	12
More active/more friends through Christianity	30	29	24
Now socialise only with born-again Christians	27	0	0
Ostracised by family and friends	23	0	0
Used to smoke - no longer smoke	17	18	6
Used to go to movies - no longer	17	12	0
Used to be wild - no longer wild	17	0	0
Relationship with family improved	13	6	0
Changes due to circumstances	3	24	71
Other changes	10	12	0
	n = 30	n = 20	n = 30

* Respondents could give more than one response

NCC = New church charismatics
ECC = Established church charismatics
MCT = Mainline church traditionalists.

Table 28 indicates that changes for charismatics were in a predictably conservative direction with an emphasis on stopping worldly pleasures.

In order of frequency these were:

	NCC %	ECC %
Used to drink - no longer drink	50	35
Used to dance and go to parties - no longer	50	29
Used to smoke - no longer	17	18
Used to go to movies - no longer	17	12
Used to be wild - no longer wild	17	0

The following comments from new church charismatic respondents typify the kinds of changes:

- *Why fill your head with garbage* (movies) *when you can fill it with God.*

- *I changed overnight - before I used to drink, smoke and live in movies.*

- *I went up and accepted the Lord - the next day I was different, didn't want to swear or smoke.*

The majority of new church charismatic respondents said that their lives were now mainly taken up with Christian activities like home fellowship groups and that they socialised mainly with born-again Christians. This is supported by the number of extra hours per week all new church charismatics spend in structured Christian activities and also by the number of friends which they have belonging to the same church (see Table 30 p.137 and Table 31 p.139).

Approximately one quarter of the new church charismatics said that they socialised only with born-again people mainly, they said, because they did not want to be contaminated or influenced:

- *We are in the world but not of it - you can have it.*

- *Now I have sincere friends - I don't just visit for social drinking.*

- *Light and darkness don't mix.*

- *I mix more with Christians.They talk the same language, have the same interests.*

- *Other people seem uncomfortable in our presence.*

- *I stay out of the company of unbelievers - we have nothing in common.*

- *You can't relate to people who are lukewarm.*

One quarter of the new church charismatics said that they had been ostracised, condemned or ridiculed by their friends and family, while only half that number said that their friends and family were tolerant or impressed by the changes in them.   This persecutory aspect of belonging to a high-profile zealous movement provides support for Kelley's suggestion that persecution enhances commitment.

- *Old friends just fell away - they don't want to see me.*

- *My friends called me a Bible-puncher but if you're true to Christ insults don't hurt us - a lot of these people have become Christians.*

Thirty percent of the new church charismatics said that they were more socially active and had made more friends through being born-again. Thirteen percent of them said that their relationships with their spouses or families had improved.   Generally a picture emerged while interviewing new church charismatic respondents that their social and personal lives had indeed dramatically changed.   This was also true, though to a lesser extent, for the established church charismatic respondents.

8.13 MEASURES OF RELIGIOUS COMMITMENT: ACTIVITIES WHICH ENCOURAGE BELONGING AND REINFORCE MEANING

8.13.1 Church attendance (see Table 29 below)

TABLE 29: CHURCH ATTENDANCE

Percentage of respondents in each sample group who attended church:

	NCC	ECC	MCT
	%	%	%
Once a week or more often	100	90	50
Once a fortnight	0	5	7
Once a month or less often	0	5	43
	n = 30	n = 20	n = 30

NCC = New church charismatics
ECC = Established church charismatics
MCT = Mainline church traditionalists

It was found that all new church charismatic respondents in the sample attend services once a week or more often. The vast majority of the established church charismatics (90%) attend services at least once a week while only half (50%) of the mainline church traditional sample attend church at least once a week, with almost half of the mainline church traditionalists (43%) attending church once a month or less often.

8.13.2 Church-related activities (see Table 30 below)

Respondents were asked: "Apart from attending services, what other church activities are you involved in?"

While half the mainline church traditional sample (50%) spent no extra time engaged in church-related activities, very few of the new church charismatic respondents (3%) and established church charismatic respondents (10%) spent no extra time engaged in church-related activities.

The vast majority of the new church charismatic (87%) and established
church charismatic (80%) samples spent three or more hours in church-
related activities compared with 26 percent of the mainline church
traditional sample. At least half of these 'involved' people spent
more than 6 hours in church-related activities.

Time spent with the church or related activities appears therefore
to be a strong factor in reinforcing religious commitment.

TABLE 30: CHURCH-RELATED ACTIVITIES

A: HOURS PER WEEK SPENT IN CHURCH-RELATED ACTIVITIES

Percentage of respondents in each sample group who spent the following
number of hours per week in church-related activities:

	NCC	ECC	MCT
	%	%	%
No extra hours	3	10	50
0 - 2 hours	10	10	24
3 - 5 hours	44	35	13
6 - 9 hours	20	25	10
10+	23	20	3

B: NATURE OF CHURCH-RELATED ACTIVITIES

Percentage of each sample group engaged in the following activities:

	NCC	ECC	MCT
	%*	%*	%*
No extra activities apart from services	3	10	50
Home fellowship/Bible Study	**73	**61	**20
Education - Sunday school, counselling, visiting	**33	10	3
Bible College courses	**30	5	0
Women's/Men's/Youth Groups	**30	**55	**20
Leadership/preaching	27	**30	**13
Active during service: choir, usher, etc.	17	**20	10
Other	7	0	0
Practical: maintenance, teas, etc.	0	15	**17
Social events	0	15	3
Community action	0	5	**13

n = 30 n = 20 n = 30
* Respondents could give more than one response
**Denotes four most common activities for each sample group

NCC = New church charismatics
ECC = Established church charismatics
MCT = Mainline church traditionalists

The nature of activities engaged in supports Kelley's (1977) hypothesis that people are primarily interested in Group A-type activities. Table 30B reveals that the most common activity (apart from attending services) for all groups was attending a home fellowship or Bible-study group. This supports the contention that people primarily want the meaning of life to be explained to them. Home fellowship groups also provide for intimate contact with others of the same faith, thus reinforcing a sense of belonging and also reinforcing the belief system.

The new churches consciously utilise the small cell technique, modelling themselves on Dr. Paul Youggi Cho of Korea, who pastors the largest local church in the world (150 000 members).

In addition to home fellowship or Bible study groups, a common activity for all three groups was to attend either a women's, men's or youth group. This type of activity also serves to reinforce meaning and belonging with the additional reinforcement of strong identification with the same sex or age group.

For the new church charismatic group the second most common activity was of a missionary or proselytising nature: teaching in the Sunday school, counselling new converts or people with problems, or visiting the sick. This supports the contention that a high degree of religious commitment is usually associated with missionary zeal.

Many of the new church charismatic sample (30%) were attending courses at the Christian Centre Bible College. The questions regarding church-related activities were only designed to measure present activities. Had they measured past activities as well, the figure of 30 percent would have been much higher. At the Christian Centre all new converts are encouraged to attend at least one course at the Bible College before they are baptised. This 'Spiritual Growth Seminar' runs for one week culminating in water baptism at the end of the week. Many other part-time courses are offered including: 'How to be a super supernatural Christian' and 'Heal the land'.

Significantly for our hypothesis, none of the new church charismatic

sample engaged in activities involving community action. Apart from
visiting the sick, it appears that the new church charismatic sample do
not consider it to be essential to engage in Group B type activities.
Participation in community activities was low for the established church
charismatic group but among the four most common activities for the
mainline church traditional group.

8.13.3 Friendship ties

Respondents were asked how many of their five best friends belonged to
the same church as they did (see Table 31A below). More than half
of the new church charismatic sample (53%) said that four or more
of their five best friends belonged to the same church. This was in
comparison with 40 percent of the established church charismatic sample
and 13 percent of the mainline charismatic traditional sample who said
that four or more of their five best friends belonged to the same
church. Friendship ties are thus important for denoting and encouraging
religious commitment.

TABLE 31: FRIENDSHIP TIES

A. Percentage of respondents in each sample group who had
the following number out of 5 best friends belonging to the
same church as they did:

	NCC	ECC	MCT
	%	%	%
None	7	10	43
1	13	15	27
2	17	30	10
3	10	5	7
4	30	25	7
5	23	15	6

B: Percentage of respondents who said that the following
number out of 5 best friends were born-again or committed
Christians:

	NCC	ECC	MCT
	%	%	%
None	3	0	7
1	0	0	17
2	7	11	28
3	0	21	3
4	27	26	14
5	63	42	31
	n = 30	n = 20	n = 30

NCC = New church charismatics
ECC = Established church charismatics
MCT = Mainline church traditionalists

To further assess how important religious belief was in the choice of friends, respondents were asked how many of their five best friends were born-again (if they themselves were born-again) or were committed Christians if they were not born-again. The results support the contention that the more committed a person is to a belief system, the more likely it will be that he/she will choose friends of the same persuasion. Ninety percent of new church charismatic respondents had 4 out of 5 friends who were born-again compared with 68 percent of established church charismatic respondents and 45 percent of mainline church traditional respondents. These results also denote the total change in social life experienced by new church charismatic converts.

8.13.4 <u>Donations</u> (see Table 32 below)

The amount of money donated to church is some indication of the degree of commitment a person feels. Respondents were asked how much money they gave to the church per month (including tithes and offerings during services).

TABLE 32: <u>DONATIONS</u>

Percentage of respondents in each sample group who donated the following amounts of money to the church:

	NCC %	ECC %	MCT %
Nothing	3	6	33
R0 - 19	17	22	47
R20 - 99	31	33	20
R100 - 199	28	17	0
R200+	21	22	0
	n = 30	n = 20	n = 30

NCC = New church charismatics
ECC = Established church charismatics
MCT = Mainline church traditionalists

Almost half the new church charismatic sample (49%) gave R100 or more
compared with 39 percent of the established church charismatic sample
and 0 percent of the mainline church traditional sample for the same
amount.   The incomes of the three groups were comparable (see Table
59, p. 196).

59 percent of the new church charismatic sample had incomes
exceeding R1 000 per month.

44 percent of the established church charismatic sample had
incomes exceeding R1 000 per month.

56 percent of the mainline church traditional sample had
incomes exceeding R1 000 per month.

In addition to indicating greater commitment, new church charismatics
give more money to the church than both established church charismatic
and mainline church traditional groups because of the new church
charismatic group's faith in the prosperity message.   Despite the
fact that mainline traditional respondents do not consider tithing
to be imperative, the amount of money donated by the mainline church
traditional group is significantly lower.   Eighty percent of the
mainline church traditional group gave R20 or less to the church
compared with 20 percent of the new church charismatic sample and
28 percent of the established church charismatic sample.

8.13.5 Reading patterns (see Table 33 below)

Ninety seven percent of new church charismatic and 100 percent of
established church charismatic respondents read the Bible once a
day or more compared with only 27 percent of mainline church charismatic
respondents.   This is consistent with exhortations by new church pastors
to *'get the Word in you'*, and claims by new church charismatic respondents
that once born-again they developed a *'hunger for the Word'*.   The majority
of charismatic respondents (new church charismatics 70% and established
church charismatics 75%) read other religious literature regularly. Up to
this point a picture emerges of a deeply committed charismatic sample.

TABLE 33: READING PATTERNS

A: Percentage of respondents in each sample group who said
    that they read the Bible:

	NCC	ECC	MCT
	%	%	%
Once a day or more often	97	100	27
Once a week	3	0	17
Occasionally/never	0	0	56

B: READING OF OTHER RELIGIOUS LITERATURE:

Percentage of respondents in each sample group who said
that they read other religious literature regularly:

NCC	ECC	MCT
%	%	%
70	75	27

C: SECULAR READING

Percentage of respondents in each sample group who
regularly read the following:

	NCC	ECC	MCT
	%	%	%
Newspapers	40	75	90
Magazines	37	55	66
Novels	20	45	57
Non-fiction	7	30	37

n = 30 n = 20 n = 30

NCC = New church charismatics
ECC = Established church charismatics
MCT = Mainline church traditionalists

Kelley (1977) speaks of fanaticism as consisting of a closed meaning

system with only selected information coming in and most communication
with non-believers being a one-way flow, outwards.   The fanaticism
of the new church charismatic respondents was evident from their
reading patterns, (see Table 33C).   A significant result emerged
when respondents were asked about reading novels.   Although 80 percent
of the new church charismatic sample said that they did not read novels
regularly, more than half of this non-reading group (60%) said that
they had been avid readers before they had been saved.   Thirty six
percent of the non-readers in the new church charismatic group volunteered this information and none of the non-readers in the mainline
church traditional group.

Their reasons for no longer reading novels were generally that they
did not have time or that they did not want to be contaminated by
"*junk*".   Taken in conjunction with changes in social life, reduced
contact with worldly activities and worldly people, it can safely
be deduced that the information which new church charismatics
are allowing themselves to receive is being voluntarily drastically
reduced.

8.13.6 Religious commitment in terms of meaning and belonging theories

On all obvious measures of religious commitment, new church charismatic
respondents were more committed than established church charismatic
respondents who were more committed than mainline church traditional
respondents.   In terms of Kelley's (1975) evidences of social
strength and concomitant traits of strictness: absolutism, discipline,
conformity, missionary zeal and fanaticism, new church charismatic
respondents indicated that they belong to a socially strong, strict
church.

Absolutism is evident from new church charismatic respondents ' adherence
to fundamentalist beliefs and their conviction that they have the monopoly
on truth.   Discipline (i.e. willingness to accept the authority of
church leadership) is implicit in the uncritical belief that the new
church leaders preach the truth although respondents were generally

careful to point out that they did not accept what anyone said unless it had Biblical support. Dissent is not tolerated by the new churches, rebelling and causing division being the principal basis for expelling a member.

It was noted during interviews with new church charismatic respondents that there was conformity, not only in the nature of responses but in the actual language used. There is a greater degree of conformity amongst new church charismatics in terms of lifestyle, beliefs and attitudes than amongst other groups. The new church charismatics do not, unlike older sectarian churches, insist on strictness or conformity of dress. The new churches are remarkably adaptive to the needs and norms of modern day society and the lack of strictness regarding dress is indicative of this.

Missionary zeal among new church charismatic respondents was obvious to interviewers. In fact many (70%) of them used the opportunity to try and convert the interviewers. Many of the new church charismatic group stated that they had agreed to the interviews in order to have an opportunity to witness and to give their testimonies. By contrast only 15 percent of the established church charismatic group and none of the mainline church traditional group tried to convert the interviewers.

Fanaticism was evident from the reading patterns of the new church charis-matic group. Apart from religious literature which would reinforce the closed system of meaning, the new church charismatic group read much less than other groups. A striking feature of interviews with new church charismatic respondents was their absolute conviction that they had now found the truth. Questions which challenged this view were un-failingly repudiated:

- *It's not what I think it's what I know.*

8.14 THE EFFECTIVENESS OF THE VARIOUS CHURCHES

As has previously been discussed, most respondents, regardless of their
religious affiliation, consider it to be greatly important for the church
to do the following: (See Graph 1, p. 97.)

 Win people to Christ

 Give inspiration and joy in worship

 Provide freedom of worship

 Give Bible instruction

 Get back to simple Bible truths

 Provide clear answers in this complex modern world

 Provide fellowship and a sense of belonging

 Help people overcome fear and anxiety

 Minister to and help people with problems

 Teach meekness and humility

 Help the needy

Most respondents regardless of their religious affiliation consider it
to be of secondary importance, or undesirable for the church to involve
itself with social justice issues.   (See Table 16, p.96 .)

Some insight into how effectively the various churches are fulfilling
the needs of their members was obtained by asking respondents how
satisfied they were with their churches.   (See Table 34 below.)

TABLE 34:   DEGREE OF SATISFACTION WITH PRESENT CHURCH

Percentage of respondents in each sample group who said
they were:

	NCC %	ECC %	MCT %
Completely satisfied	80	65	31
Somewhat satisfied	17	35	45
Uncertain	0	0	7
Somewhat dissatisfied	3	0	14
Completely dissatisfied	0	0	3
	n = 30	n = 20	n = 30

NCC = New church charismatics
ECC = Established church charismatics
MCT = Mainline church traditionalists

Members of the new churches are, according to these results,
far more satisfied with their church than established church respondents,
while the established church charismatic respondents are relatively far
more satisfied than their mainline church traditionalist counterparts.

8.14.1 Why the new churches are successful

New church charismatic respondents were asked a number of questions designed to measure what it is that the new churches are providing that
is making them so successful. The questions were open-ended and consisted of the following: "What encouraged you to join the Christian
Centre?" (Table 35); "What makes you completely satisfied?" (Table 36) and
"What have you found at the Christian Centre that you did not find in
your previous church?" (Table 37).

TABLE 35:

FACTORS ENCOURAGING NEW CHURCH CHARISMATICS TO JOIN THE
NEW CHURCHES

Percentage of sample who gave the following reasons:

	%*
The teaching of the truth and quality of speakers/preachers	90
The presence, move or leadership of the Holy Spirit	47
The fellowship and sense of belonging	43
The free and joyful worship	33
The healing and miracles	30
Change in significant person/family unity	17
.Life crisis	13
The reality of Satan	10
Greater sincerity/more conviction/involvement	10

* Respondents could give more than one response

TABLE 36: REASONS FOR COMPLETE SATISFACTION WITH CHURCH

Percentage of respondents in each sample group who gave the following reasons:

	NCC %*	ECC %*	MCT %*
Teaching is sound, clear, truth, based on the Bible	63	60	14
Worship and praise is free/joyful/ sincere/informal	53	20	21
Good fellowship/companionship/ sense of belonging	37	40	14
Flowing with God/moving with the Holy Spirit	33	15	0
Spiritual growth encouraged - guidance and courses provided	27	5	10
All needs satisfied	23	15	17
See evidence of the power and presence of God	20	15	0
Other reasons	13	25	28
Not completely satisfied	20	35	69
	n = 30	n = 20	n = 30

NCC = New church charismatics
ECC = Established church charismatics
MCT = Mainline church traditionalists

*Respondents could give more than one response

TABLE 37: FEATURES FOUND AT NEW CHURCH NOT FOUND AT PREVIOUS CHURCH

Percentage of sample who named the following features:

	%*
Free, joyful worship	57
Holy Spirit moving/controlling - gifts of Holy Spirit	53
Sincere relationship with Jesus - love, joy	43
Evidence of power and presence of God	33
Teaching of truth - good preaching and pastors	27
Commitment/total involvement	23
Fellowship/love/community	20
	n = 30

* Respondents could give more than one response

In summary, the most common positive features of the new churches as
stated by new church charismatic respondents were as follows:

Sound teaching and teachers/preachers

The presence and power of the Holy Spirit

Free joyful worship

Fellowship

Commitment

Genuine relationship with Jesus

When compared with what all respondents want from church it appears
that the new churches are providing what many people need (i.e. Kelley's
(1977) Group A type activities).

8.14.1.1 Sound teaching and teachers

This category includes all responses which referred to either the con-
tent of the teachings of the new churches or the teachers/preachers
themselves or their style of delivery. The most common responses in
this category were unequivocal statements referring to the conviction
that the new churches were preaching the truth or that their teachings
were based on the Bible. Typical responses were as follows:

- *Everything is done correctly according to the Bible.*
- *They know what truth is.*
- *We choose to believe God rather than man.*
- *You learn something every time.*
- *They gave it to us much better.*
- *They knew what they were and what they were doing.*
- *Everything he said hit me right between the eyes.*
- *It's in line with the Word of God – they teach the Word.*
- *All my questions are being answered.*
- *The Bible says 'My people perish through lack of knowledge'.
  The mainline churches don't know God's promises – here we learn
  about God's promises.*

- *You have teachers who have travelled world-wide and have experience in teaching - we have international speakers coming regularly.*
- *The teachings are solid and completely backed by the Bible.*
- *They are led by God not man.*
- *It gives a more powerful message. It also gives more meaning to the Christian faith.*
- *I liked what I heard at the Christian Centre - no social gospel - it was the word of God.*

8.14.1.2 The presence and power of the Holy Spirit

Responses in this category referred to the fact that respondents felt that the new churches are moved by the Holy Spirit and allowing the Holy Spirit the freedom to work. Many respondents referred to the power which the Holy Spirit has and frees. It was clear from the kinds of responses in this category, that visible evidence of the Holy Spirit was very important to respondents. This supports the high percentage of new church charismatic respondents who agreed that it is the church's task to provide signs and wonders and miracles. (See Table 16, p. 96.)

Typical responses in this category were as follows:

- *They are free to move as the spirit leads them.*
- *You come for heart appeasement like a petrol tank. It has given me a lot more confidence - I've become much stronger - it's exhilarating.*
- *To live without the Holy Spirit you are dead. The Holy Spirit shows me things every day - it's not luck or intuition.*
- *It was almost like the Holy Spirit was wooing me.*
- *Total obedience to the leading of the Holy Spirit.*
- *With tongues came power, strength and courage to take any knock.*
- *Being spirit-filled is the power to live the Christian life.*
- *I saw the supernatural at work.*
- *The praise and worship is powerful.*
- *You can see the evidence that God is really leading the church - evidence of prayers being answered.*

- *You can see that it's a living Word.*
- *I felt the presence of God - something tangible.*
- *You see the Holy Spirit being allowed to control a meeting.*
- *You could see people falling as the pastor blew - it's wonderful to see the Holy Spirit at work.*

Many new church charismatic respondents referred specifically to the power and authority which they now had as a result of being spirit-filled:

- *I used to just accept things before and say it was God's will.*
- *Now I know I can do whatever I want.*
- *The Holy Spirit is God's power on earth - till the rapture comes the Holy Spirit is here and will teach you to do things to glorify Jesus.*
- *You can't be a failure - you're a conqueror.*
- *The whole time I was reading the Bible all I saw was power power power.*
- *I'm much more confident - nothing is impossible.*
- *I'm a conqueror and victorious. I'm reigning with Jesus.*
- *Through serving Him He's in you - you feel like you've got the whole kingdom of God - the power of the universe within you.*
- *They believe you should be victorious all the time as a Christian.*
- *I'm not alone and I have the Lord's power.*
- *The power in Christianity is in the Baptism of the Holy Spirit - then one has power within to overcome a lot more.*
- *We are like receiving dynamos - we receive the power that works miracles.*

8.14.1.3 Joyful free worship

It was clear from responses that this feature of the new churches was very important to new church charismatic respondents. Many of them referred to the honest, open, sincere worship and to how good it made them feel. Typical responses were as follows:

- *I love the freedom of worshipping and praising – to dance and sing and get lost in His presence.*
- *You must worship in spirit and truth.*
- *I have the freedom – if God tells me to do something I can do it.*
- *I come out of the service feeling that I've gained something.*
- *I like to feel glorious and happy in His Word.*
- *Dancing, lifting hands, clapping – these things break bondages. You can see it a mile off on their faces.*
- *I can lose myself in God and come into His presence.*
- *It's a more liberal and honest way of expressing your love for God.*

8.14.1.4 Fellowship and love

Many respondents stated that they felt that this was a unique feature of the new churches. The intimate contact with other worshippers brought about by embracing and shaking hands was regularly referred to. Typical comments were as follows:

- *There is beautiful friendship there.*
- *I go to home fellowships because I'm hungry for food* (spiritual) *and sharing – we are loading something off our hearts.*
- *We are sheep all together so the wolf (devil) can't attack – there's power there, the power of unity.*
- *I've never experienced such love.*
- *There is tremendous blessing there – a sense of comfort and security.*

8.14.1.5 Commitment/total involvement

New church charismatic respondents typically said that they liked the new churches because they could get totally involved. They referred to what they perceived as the greater conviction of the new church pastors and they took this as evidence of greater sincerity. Typical responses were:

- *Love is more real there – there's greater sincerity there. They are doing more things for God.*

- *They don't only talk about things that are good - they do it.*
- *I could get fully involved.   There was an opportunity for me to reach out and witness.*

8.14.1.6 Genuine relationship with Jesus

New church charismatics' responses in this category generally referred to the fact that the new churches had given them their first genuine experience of a loving relationship with Jesus:

- *My old church didn't teach the love of Christ - only fear and condemnation, now I know what Christ's love is.*
- *I'd never been confronted with Jesus before.*
- *I felt the love of Christ come into my heart and flood through me.*
- *It is an experience with Jesus Christ.*
- *I know the Lord.   I go to see the Lord - the Lord is more real to me.*

8.14.1.7 The opinions of new church pastors

New church pastors were asked, "What in particular does your church offer people?"   Their replies confirmed what new church charismatic respondents said about the new churches.

- *An alive, joyful free church.*
- *A personal relationship with Jesus Christ.*
- *A return to Book of Acts Christianity.*
- *A return to the integrity and simplicity of the Bible.*
- *Greater freedom to flow with the Holy Spirit.*
- *A lifestyle that works.*
- *We teach people how to apply the Word of God, God's principles to their lives.*
- *We teach them to take God's Word and make It work.*
- *We teach people how to release the power of God within them - then they have authority and can release their full potential.*
- *Salvation every Sunday.*
- *We confront the forces of evil - the powers of darkness - the devil is alive and well.*

- *We actually preach about the infilling of the Holy Spirit and about healing.*
- *Love and commitment.*
- *Freedom in worship to move with what God wants.*

8.14.2 Opinions of clergy and theologians of established churches

Attitudes of established church clergymen and theologians interviewed towards the new churches ranged from outright condemnation, to qualified recognition that the new churches were performing a necessary evangelical function.

8.14.2.1 Criticism of faith/prosperity teachings

The chief and most common criticism was of the faith teachings of the new churches.

It was felt by theologians interviewed that the new churches had no ecclesiology or eschatology.   Regarding the prosperity or faith teachings of the new churches, criticisms in summary were as follows: The notion that prosperity (health and wealth) necessarily follows faith in Christ is rank error, naive and harmful according to established church people interviewed.   The new churches are making prosperity an end in itself instead of a by-product.   Prosperity is not a reward of faith, faithfulness or spirituality, and this teaching creates and appeals to wrong motives in people receiving the message.

The faith message, according to critics interviewed, simply becomes a way of ordering God around and manipulating him.   It becomes a 'religified version of the power of positive thinking'.   The fact that not everyone is healed or becomes financially prosperous leads to the poor and sick developing tremendous burdens of guilt because, according to the faith teachings, their faith is not strong enough or there is some hidden sin in their lives.   This can lead to a collapse of faith in God altogether.   (A number of ministers testified to having had to counsel the 'casualties' of the faith message.)   In the words of one minister *"It is certainly a cruel gospel for the one who loves Christ though confined to a cancer ward or a wheel chair"*. Because adherents of the faith message are meant to be healthy and wealthy they are forced to deny negative realities in their lives, which leads to stunting of the personality, alienation and role-playing.

8.14.2.2 Criticism of the absence of a social gospel

Most ministers and theologians interviewed were of the opinion that a great deal of the appeal of the new churches was that they did not preach or teach a social gospel. They referred to the resistance to the social gospel within their own churches, and felt that many people could not cope with the demands which being a Christian in South Africa made on them.

The new churches' explanation and treatment of suffering, they felt, was simplistic and unrealistic but was affording people an escape from the insecure and tense situation in South Africa today. The fact that the new church services are not racially segregated was giving people the illusory impression that things were changing. As one clergyman put it, *"Let's all have a happy multiracial clappy and feel better"*.

8.14.2.3 Additional criticisms

Additional criticisms made by ministers and theologians were:

- *The new churches are divisive, causing splits in churches and families.*
- *The pastors are not qualified and are hence more likely to deliver erroneous teachings.*
- *The teachings of the new churches lead to a lack of discipline in Christians.*
- *Although the new church pastors do not want to be under the authority of traditional church structures they are authoritarian within their own churches.*

8.14.2.4 Positive opinions about the new churches

Apart from qualified recognition of the evangelical endeavours of the
new churches, some clergy felt that for young people particularly, the
new churches were providing a simple, tangible, transforming, personalised
religion as opposed to the sometimes remote, unreal, intangible God
presented in the established churches.   A Pentecostal minister interviewed said that older Pentecostal churches were losing their appeal
because of their anti-worldliness.   The casual dress, modern music
and prosperity message of the new churches was overcoming this un-
attractive aspect of Pentecostalism and was more appealing, particularly
to young people.

The firm conviction of the new churches that God still works in extra-
ordinary ways was acknowledged as a positive feature by some clerics.

8.14.3 Attitudes of established church respondents towards the new churches

In view of the fact that many established church respondents were not
completely satisfied with their present church (see Table 34, p.145)
one could assume that they would be potential converts to the new
churches.   Respondents were asked,"Do you ever feel that you might
want to join one of the newer non-denominational churches?"   (See
Table 38 below.)

TABLE 38:   DESIRE TO JOIN THE NEW CHURCHES

Percentage of respondents in non-new church sample
who stated that they:

	ECC %	MCT %
Would definitely like to join the new churches	0	3
Would like to join new churches (with reservation)	5	4
Did not know about the new churches	5	0
Would not like to join but saw good points	45	20
Would definitely not like to join the new churches	45	73
	n = 20	n = 30

ECC = Established church charismatics
MCT = Mainline church traditionalists

Table 38 reveals that very few established church respondents (5% of
established church charismatic respondents and 7% of mainline church
traditional respondents) said that they would definitely like to join
a new church. However, a significant proportion of established church
charismatic respondents (45%) said that although they did not want to
join a new church they saw positive features in these churches. The
majority of mainline church traditional respondents (73%) said that
they would definitely not like to join a new church and identified
mainly negative features. The difference in attitude between
established church charismatic and mainline church traditional respondents is predictable in view of the charismatic features of the
new churches.

Positive statements about the new churches (see Table 39 below) were
fairly uniform, the most common being that the new churches were doing
a good job evangelically (saving souls), that they were healing
people, and that the worship and praise at the new churches was free
and joyful. Some established church charismatic respondents voiced
the opinion that the new churches were filling a gap left by established churches by ministering to peoples' needs. A few respondents
(5% of established church charismatic respondents and 7% of mainline
church traditional respondents) were impressed by the non-denominationalism of the new churches.

TABLE 39: POSITIVE STATEMENTS ABOUT THE NEW CHURCHES

Percentage of respondents in established churches who made the
following statements concerning the new churches:

	ECC	MCT
	%*	%*
No positive statements made	40	70
New churches doing a good job - saving souls/ healing	30	11
Worship and praise free and joyful	30	11
New churches doing a good job - ministering to peoples' needs	20	4
Non-denominationalism good	5	7
Other positive statements	5	7
	n = 20	n = 30

ECC = Established church charismatics
MCT = Mainline church traditionalists

* Respondents could give more than one response

Table 40 below illustrates that criticisms of the new churches far outweighed positive statements about them. The most common criticism made by established church charismatic respondents was that the new church pastors were unqualified and that certain of the teachings (commonly prosperity and healing) were unsound. The most common criticism made by mainline church traditional respondents and by a substantial number of established church charismatic respondents was that they disliked what they called the exuberance, emotionalism or hysteria of the new churches. A common criticism made by both mainline church traditional and established church charismatic respondents was that the new churches were insincere, shallow, superficial, showy or escapist.

TABLE 40: NEGATIVE STATEMENTS ABOUT THE NEW CHURCHES - REASONS FOR NOT WANTING TO JOIN NEW CHURCHES

Percentage of respondents in established church sample who made the following statements concerning the new churches:

	ECC %*	MCT %*
No negative statements made	10	15
Needs supplied by own church	25	15
Prefer security, permanence, discipline, authority and calm of traditional church	25	**22
Dislike exuberance, emotionalism, hysteria	**30	**48
New churches insincere, shallow, superficial, showy, escapist	**30	**41
New church pastors unqualified, teaching unsound	**60	15
New churches too pressurising, manipulative, threatening	15	11
Loyal to own denomination	15	11
Other reasons (including new churches too rigid, too authoritarian, divisive, ignore wider social issues)	15	15
	n = 20	n = 30

ECC = Established church charismatics
MCT = Mainline church traditionalists

* Respondents could give more than one response
** Indicates 3 most common opinions for each sample group

The following were typical criticisms made by established church respondents:

- *Their whole religious belief rests on miracles. I question it's validity - people get born-again but often it doesn't last.*
- *I can't believe that they call themselves Christians, because of the values they have.*
- *I had a very good friend who joined them - within 6 months he had become the most intolerable bigot I've ever met.*
- *They are escapist - I'm suspicious about the mass hysteria.*
- *I hate all the kissing and clapping - I'm much too reserved for that.*
- *Those who join are shallow - looking for sensation without deep commitment.*
- *They are removing themselves from the realities of life.*
- *I got the willies when I went - it was a terrifying experience - mass hysteria.*
- *They have an ostrich attitude - they haven't come to grips with what their black brothers are thinking.*
- *They often show lack of love, exclusivity and condemnation of other Christians.*

8.14.4 Attitudes towards the mainline churches

New church respondents feel that the new churches are fulfilling certain needs (see 8.14.1). By implication other churches are, according to the new church charismatic sample not providing what the new churches are providing. That is, other churches are:

not allowing free joyful worship

not allowing the Holy Spirit to move

not providing opportunities for the manifestation of God's power

not developing or encouraging a personal relationship with Jesus

not providing good teaching

not encouraging total involvement

not providing fellowship

To check whether these criticisms were actively felt by the new church charismatic group and not just implied, and whether these criticisms were felt by all respondents, respondents were asked why they had left their previous churches (see Table 41), and what criticisms they had of the mainline churches in general (see Table 42).

Table 41 below reveals that the most common reason for leaving their previous church given by all three sample groups was that their previous church had been dead, dry and boring. This criticism is therefore not unique to the new church charismatic group. It appears that, regardless of religious affiliation, people generally, as a priority, want services to be alive, stimulating and relevant. They are actually leaving churches which are not satisfying them in this regard. Another reason given by all three groups for leaving was a lack of love,fellowship and community. This confirms the theory that fellowship and a sense of belonging are needs felt by most respondents.

TABLE 41:   REASONS FOR LEAVING PREVIOUS CHURCH

Percentage of respondents in each sample group who gave the following reasons:

	NCC %*	ECC %*	MCT %*
Too traditional, dead, boring, dry	**63	**41	**20
Not moving with the Holy Spirit/don't preach the Holy Spirit	**40	12	0
Jesus/love/reality of relationship not preached	**30	0	0
Salvation not preached/insisted upon	23	0	0
Commitment not expected or needed	23	6	0
The truth/the word not taught	20	6	0
Healing not practised or believed in	17	0	0
Water baptism not practised	10	0	0
No love, fellowship or community	10	**12	**4
Did not help with problems	10	0	3
Circumstantial	10	**18	**7
Too political or intellectual	7	0	0
Other reasons (personal)	13	30	24
Did not leave - still same church	3	29	59

                              n = 30 n = 20 n = 30

NCC = New church charismatics
ECC = Established church charismatics
MCT = Mainline church traditionalists

** Indicates the 3 most common reasons for leaving
* Respondents could give more than one reason

Certain reasons for leaving were confined to charismatics (i.e. the
new church charismatic and established church charismatic group).
In view of previous discussion these are predictable:

- the church was not preaching the Holy Spirit or moving
  with it

- commitment/total involvement was not expected or needed,
  the whole truth/'Word' was not taught

A reason given only by the new church charismatic sample and mainline
church traditional sample was that their previous church had not
helped them when they had had a particular problem.

Some of the reasons for leaving were peculiar or exclusive to the new
church charismatic sample.   These referred to the fact that other
churches did not enable or preach a real and loving relationship with
Jesus, did not preach or insist upon a salvational experience, did
not practise or believe in healing and water baptism, and that they
were too political or intellectual.   All of these reasons support
the contention that new church charismatics want and are getting an
immediate, personal, dramatic experience of religion with no inter-
ference from other secondary issues like wider social concerns.

TABLE 42: CRITICISMS OF MAINLINE CHURCHES IN GENERAL

Percentage of respondents in each sample group who made the
following criticisms:

	NCC %*	ECC %*	MCT %*
Too traditional, dead, meaningless	**87	**50	**27
Not teaching, recognising, moving with Holy Spirit	**60	**20	0
Whole truth/Word not preached, misinterpreted	**20	**25	0
Denominationalism, factionalism, disunity	**20	**25	**23
Lack commitment, relevance, direction	17	15	13
Neglect youth/only cater for old people	17	5	3
Neglect reality of relationship with Jesus	13	10	0
Not evangelical enough/don't emphasise salvation	13	15	0
Don't believe in water baptism and baptism of the Holy Spirit	13	5	0
Too political	13	**20	**33
Don't emphasise reality of Satan	3	0	0
Other criticisms (personal)	7	20	40
No criticisms	3	10	27
	n = 30	n = 20	n = 30

NCC = New church charismatics
ECC = Established church charismatics
MCT = Mainline church traditionalists
 * Respondents could give more than one response
** Indicates 3 most common criticisms made by each sample group

Table 42 supports the inferences made about the mainline churches thus
far. Most respondents were hesitant about criticising the mainline
churches and prefaced their criticisms with some sort of apology to
the effect that they were sure the mainline churches were sincere and
doing their misguided best.

Nevertheless the criticisms which emerged were consistent with the

implications thus far.   All sample groups said that the mainline churches
were too concerned with tradition and that sermons were dead and meaningless.   This criticism was predictably made most often by the new church
charismatic group, followed by the established church charismatic group,
with the mainline church traditionalist group making this criticism least
often.

Other criticisms made by all groups were that there was too much
factionalism and disunity amongst the mainline churches who were far
too interested in their own particular denomination.   It appears
that non-denominationalism is attractive to people regardless of their
religious affiliation.   A great deal of the appeal of the new churches
may lie in their claim to non-demoninationalism.

Another criticism voiced by all sample groups was that the mainline
churches lacked commitment, direction and relevance and that they
tended to neglect the youth and only cater for older people.

All groups commonly said that the mainline churches were too political.
Surprisingly for our results thus far, the mainline church traditionalist
group made this criticism more often than other groups and this was in
fact the most common criticism of mainline churches made by the mainline
church traditional sample group (33%).   This could be due to the fact
that the mainline church traditional respondents are most exposed to the
social gospel while for the new church charismatic sample, it is no
longer an issue, merely an unpleasant memory.

Typical responses concerning political issues by new church charismatic
respondents were:

- *They pray for blacks but wouldn't pray for a hurt child.*
- *They preach politics and get in trouble.*
- *I found the sermons boring - social gospel - rarely heard
  Jesus Christ or Holy Spirit exalted - things they told me
  to do I could never do of my own volition.   The social kick
  was not my idea of being a Christian because I knew I couldn't
  do it because I didn't have the strength, inclination, desire
  or the hunger.*

- *They have to channel their frustrations into the social gospel because they have no manifestations.*

Mainline church traditional respondents made the following kinds of comments regarding the 'political' involvement of the mainline churches:

- *The ones that spout politics from dawn to dusk make the church go down.*
- *They are so worried about political things - helping blacks that they couldn't be bothered with someone sick in their own parish.*
- *They don't seem to be alive enough - they are too concerned with other things.*
- *Continual harping on politics irritates people.*
- *It's not for the leaders to stampede people into something.*
- *For what must I kiss the bishop's ring when he says things like that.*

Once again, certain criticisms were made only by the charismatics in the sample. These followed the by now predictable pattern of neglect of the Holy Spirit, misinterpretation or inadequate preaching of the Bible, neglecting to establish a genuine relationship with Jesus and neglecting to emphasise salvation or to be evangelical.

As our concern is chiefly with new churches, a range of criticisms made by new church charismatic respondents about the mainline churches follows:

- *They are too complacent - not leading people into a relationship with God but into a form of death.*
- *Religion kills the gospel alive - there are too many do's and don'ts.*
- *Learnt nothing there.*
- *They are in bondage because of man-made rules.*
- *They just don't get down to what it's all about - they don't preach salvation and eternal life.*
- *They deny the power of God - God won't move and the church won't grow.*
- *They are just trying to keep congregations happy and to cover up uncertainty in the Word - there's a set of rules in there - tithes, water baptism, speaking in tongues, which they are avoiding.*

- *They are blinded by the prince of this world - they can't understand the truth of the Word because they are not born-again.*
- *They don't have the spirit of God energising and quickening them.*
- *They lack the reality of the living Christ - it's just history being taught.*
- *There is not enough stress on fulfilment now.*
- *They don't preach the word of God in total truth.*
- *The church never brought me into any full commitment.*

Unfortunately many of these criticisms by respondents are made in hindsight. They could not have been the reasons for leaving at the time. The only criticisms which appear to have pertained at the time of exit were:

too traditional, dead and meaningless

neglect of youth

too political.

The criticisms of the mainline churches depend to a certain extent on whether respondents are charismatic or not. However when respondents who were not completely satisfied with their present church were asked why they were not completely satisfied (see Table 43 below), and when all respondents were asked whether and why it was necessary to attend church (see Table 44 below), certain common needs emerged which once again confirm our findings thus far.

People go to church for the fellowship, sharing, teaching, guidance and encouragement and are dissatisfied when the church does not fulfil these requirements.

TABLE 43: REASONS WHY NOT COMPLETELY SATISFIED

Percentage of respondents in each sample group who were dissatisfied for the following reasons:

	NCC %*	ECC %*	MCT %*
Too traditional, hierarchical, factional	0	20	14
Congregation not involved, committed	0	15	18
No recognition of Holy Spirit	0	10	4
Dissatisfied with sermons/minister/leadership	7	5	14
Too political	0	5	7
Limited social/political awareness	0	5	7
Lack of fellowship/belonging/caring	7	0	14
Own fault	0	0	14
Other reasons (personal)	7	5	14
Completely satisfied	80	65	32
	n = 30	n = 20	n = 30

NCC = New church charismatics
ECC = Established church charismatics
MCT = Mainline church traditionalists

* Respondents could give more than one response

TABLE 44:   REASONS WHY IT IS NECESSARY TO ATTEND CHURCH

Percentage of respondents in each sample group who said that
attending church was necessary for the following reasons:

	NCC %*	ECC %*	MCT %*
Need the fellowship and assembling together	68	86	46
Need the teaching	23	50	31
Need the 'spiritual food'/encouragement	27	14	31
Need communal worship/prayer power	23	29	31
Need the sharing and giving	9	36	15
Other reasons	5	0	8
	n = 30	n = 20	n = 30

NCC = New church charismatics
ECC = Established church charismatics
MCT = Mainline church traditionalists

* Respondents could give more than one response

8.14.5 Attitudes of new church pastors towards the mainline churches

Although the new church pastors interviewed were initially hesitant
about condemning the mainline churches outright, the general consensus
was that they were not moving with the Holy Spirit and were thus getting
left behind.

Apart from criticising the constraints of traditional church structures
and traditions, the pastors interviewed criticised the established
churches for not following 'the Word' in the following areas: water
baptism, the infilling of the Holy Spirit, healing and miracles, and
prosperity, and for preaching politics from the pulpit.   Typical
responses were:

- *God is not in a box.*
- *People in mainline churches are just hearing stories, they*
  are not getting fed.

- *People don't want to hear politics, they want to hear the Word of God and how to apply it to their lives.*
- *The mainline churches are not acting on what God says - you can't just take out bits that suit you.*
- *They haven't recognised the common enemy Satan who is destroying peoples' lives.*
- *Mainline churches haven't taught people how to operate in God's principles - how to live with God's power in them.*
- *The churches are dead - they aren't moving where God is moving.*
- *They don't encourage people to look at the Bible.*
- *People are being spiritually stunted in the mainline churches.*
- *The main reason people are leaving is because of the liberal social gospel - people don't want money to go to the World Council of Churches to pay for terrorists to kill their sons on the borders.*
- *They don't teach the faith message: How can a prayer of faith be 'Thy will be done'.*

The new church pastors interviewed said that they had no quarrel with the mainline churches and were not 'sheep-stealing' or trying to break them down. They felt that Christians were all part of the same family and that they were simply trying to do what God wanted them to do. The general impression gained from pastors was that the mainline churches were anti them rather than vice versa. In view of their criticisms of mainline churches, the protestations of tolerance seem inaccurate.

Fred Roberts (in Channel Jan./Feb. 1983, p.20) who is the most influential new church pastor in Durban states: "I used to tell people, 'Go back to your church and bring revival to your church'. Now I tell them 'If your church is dead, leave it!'"

In the Pinetown area there is an attempt at reconciliation between churches in the Minister's Fraternal called Here's Life Highway, an association of established church clergy and new church pastors who meet on a social basis once a month. The objectives of Here's Life Highway are the healing and strengthening of the body, to build trust and relationship between leaders of the various churches and to be supportive and pray

for each other.   Doctrinal differences between the new churches
and   established churches have not seriously been confronted, the
emphasis being more on fellowship.

CHAPTER 9

CONCLUSIONS

9.1 RESUMÉ OF MOST SIGNIFICANT FINDINGS

Because of the size and nature of the sample, the findings of this survey are necessarily tentative.   However, certain trends emerged fairly consistently and unambiguously throughout the survey and it is these trends which require consideration and comment as they raise important issues.

Fear of the future and insecurity

We have found that most respondents in the sample perceive the world, and possibly South Africa particularly, as dangerous and threatening.   It has been suggested that one of the primary reasons that the new churches are popular is because they are allaying peoples' fears.   Although most new church charismatic respondents felt that it was natural for people in general to fear the future in this country, they denied that they themselves feared the future.   A large proportion of new church charismatic respondents said that they felt much more confident and secure than they felt before they were born-again and a large proportion reported that they were much less anxious than they had previously been.

Powerlessness

The literature concerning the growth of new religious movements suggests that status deprivation (powerlessness) is a primary factor in accounting for the burgeoning membership of new churches.   Certain characteristics of new church respondents in the sample suggest that the new churches are particularly appealing to those whose occupations are relatively insecure, albeit immediately financially lucrative and to those who have no clear political 'home'.   Although the mainline church traditionalist respondents in the sample perceived themselves to be

much more powerless (to affect events in the world around them) than
charismatic respondents in general, it is suggested that their security
came from more diverse sources than that of charismatic respondents
who had found their sense of control over their lives chiefly through
their church participation.   The new churches particularly, appear,
according to glowing reports of increased authority and confidence,
to be remedying the powerlessness felt by their members.

Personality types and life crises

Survey results showed that more new church charismatic respondents than
other respondents claimed to have experienced problems prior to being
'saved'.   There is therefore some suggestion that the new churches are
appealing to people with problems or particular personality types, i.e.
those who tend to be anxious, neurotic or 'hysterical' (in the psycho-
analytic sense).   However there seems little benefit in 'writing off'
the new churches as appealing only to cranks and misfits in view of the
fact that our survey results show that similar problems were and
are experienced by many of the respondents regardless of their
religious affiliations.

Authoritarianism, dogmatism and reliance on an external source of authority

Responses to various statements designed to measure authoritarianism and
related characteristics suggest that new church charismatic respondents
tend to reveal more authoritarian responses than their established church
counterparts.   The majority of all charismatic respondents were sure that
they had found the meaning and purpose of life.   This positive, confident
perception of life must however be weighed against its concomitants which
appear to be dogmatism and fanaticism.   Interviewers consistently
noted the absolute conviction of new church charismatic respondents
that they were right and had found the truth.   Questions or probes
which suggested alternative points of view were treated with genuine
surprise that anyone could be so foolish as not to have seen the error
of these viewpoints.   Dogmatism does not correlate well with or encourage questioning and investigation.   The fact that the vast majority
of new church charismatic respondents consider that it is the devil who

plants doubt and uncertainty in peoples' minds encourages an even greater aversion to critical thinking. The fact that almost all new church charismatic respondents consider it correct that people should submit (without question) to those placed in authority over them confirms the impression that new church charismatic respondents display classic authoritarian features. This is perhaps best reflected by the comment from a new church charismatic respondent who, when confronted with a perplexing moral question said: *"I don't really know - we've still got to learn about that"*.

It is suggested that while new church charismatic respondents may have been more authoritarian than 'average' prior to joining the new churches, the teachings of the new churches are enhancing the authoritarian tendencies or traits of their members.

Political conservatism

The survey results show that new church charismatics are more politically conservative than their established church counterparts in voting patterns, racial and general political attitudes (e.g. opinions concerning conscientious objection). The fact that the large majority of new church charismatic respondents reported that their political attitudes had changed since being born-again suggests that the new churches are actively influencing their members' political attitudes, particularly by encouraging a very dismissive attitude to political issues. This influence is subtle in some respects and obvious in others: obvious in terms of their adherence to a literal interpretation of Romans 13 and their total rejection of the social gospel, and subtle in that members are led to believe that they do enough in the South African context because their services are multiracial and blacks are being 'saved'. They are satisfied that this proves that the Lord is indeed moving mightily in this country and that nothing else needs to be done.

This attitude gives a false sense of optimism and complacency regarding the future of this country, perhaps best exemplified by one new church charismatic respondent, who did not want her sons to go to 'the border' and when asked how this could be avoided said: *"I'm going to put my sons in varsity till Jesus comes"*.

Attitudes towards suffering, prosperity and poverty

New church charismatic respondents showed that they believe almost unanimously that innocent suffering is the work of the devil, with a large proportion believing that the devil specifically causes poverty, physical illness and psychological problems. By contrast most mainline church traditional respondents say that they do not understand the cause of innocent suffering although they are sure that God does not want people to suffer. While this is indicative of a humble recognition of the complexity of the enigma of innocent suffering, it nevertheless illustrates that part of the appeal of the new churches is that they provide absolute explanations for complex and diverse phenomena.

The results show that new church charismatic respondents accept the prosperity message as elucidated by Hagin (1980) and Copeland (1974). They believe that God wants people to be financially prosperous and that the reason for giving is to get back. The obverse of this is that poor people are outside of God's ambit and are, to some extent, to blame for permitting the devil to have such an influence over their lives. This attitude towards the poor and to suffering in general has the most serious implications for traditional notions of Christian compassion and responsibility. The explanation of suffering is erroneous, simplistic, and encourages contempt for the poor and abandonment of responsibility towards them.

What people want from church

It is clear from the results of this survey that people want an immediate and gratifying experience when they go to church and that they are often not getting this from the established churches. Also, certain people want the church to give them clear and simple answers, to cope with the complexity and threat of the world around them.

Our results have shown that all respondents consistently and unanimously rated certain activities as being of primary importance for the church. These were: winning people to Christ, helping the needy, ministering to and helping people with their problems, giving Bible instruction, getting back to simple Bible truths and providing fellowship and a sense of belonging. In addition more than 80 percent of the total sample felt it important that the church should: give inspiration and joy in worship, provide freedom of worship, help people to overcome fear and anxiety, teach meekness and humility, and give clear answers in this complex modern world.

According to the results of this survey, new church charismatic respondents are completely satisfied with their church for the following reasons: new churches are teaching 'the truth', the Holy Spirit is allowed to work freely, the worship is free and joyful, it encourages a genuine relationship with Jesus and there is sincere fellowship and love in the congregation. Apart from the absence of any mention of meekness and humility it appears that the new churches are providing what many people want.

By contrast our results show that mainline church traditional respondents are generally only somewhat satisfied with their churches. Their criticisms, in summary, are that their churches are too concerned with tradition, they are dry and boring, there is not enough genuine fellowship and they are too political.

Most respondents, regardless of their church affiliation, rate church involvement in broader social issues to be less important than what they consider to be the primary tasks of the church to be: serving and attending to the needs of their own members, and evangelising. New church charismatics strongly reject the social gospel as a distortion of the Christian message. This view is consistent with their somewhat greater political conservatism. But, significantly, mainline church traditionalists are themselves unenthusiastic about the social gospel. Their most common criticism of their churches is that too much emphasis is placed on 'politics' and social concerns.

One conclusion which may be drawn from the above, although erroneous and simplistic, has a ring of truth to it, viz. that less politics should be preached in the mainline churches. A better explanation is that the common method of dealing with social issues may be such as to provoke some antagonism and resentment. It seems that information regarding the suffering of the masses is emphasised, and there is an implied criticism and attack on the church members, as if they are to be blamed for the unhappy plight of the black majority. This is an unjustifiable burden upon a congregation. The average white church-goer should not be blamed for the injustices and horrors of apartheid. He or she should not be made to feel guilty for the consequences of the unjust system in which we live. Rather, social explanation should focus on historical causes of political and economic inequalities, and, as far as possible, participation by a congregation in justice and reconciliation should be a joyful and purposeful activity, free of guilt and self-reproach.

9.2 ASSESSMENT OF THE NEW CHURCHES

There can be no doubt that the new churches are fulfilling certain needs for certain people. This is evidenced by the rapid growth of the new churches which are not only attracting substantial numbers from the conservative Pentecostal churches and Afrikaans churches like the Nederduitse Gereformeerde Kerk, but also from the more 'liberal' English churches. Many people report feeling happier, healthier, wealthier, more positive and more powerful as a result of joining the new churches. In isolation this would appear to be innocuous, if not beneficial, because peoples' lives seem to be enhanced by the confidence and sense of meaning and purpose attained through commitment to the new churches. However the more subtle influences of the new churches are serious and potentially harmful as we will suggest in due course.

The literature on the growth of new religious movements reveals that people tend to huddle when threatened, forming themselves into highly bounded   groups which perceive the world in terms of 'them' as opposed to 'us'. We suggest that the people to whom the new churches

are primarily appealing are insecure, fearful, bored members of the
lower middle class and new middle class in South Africa: insecure and
fearful because the future does not look as predictable as it did 10
years ago, and bored because they are powerless even though they have
certain advantages.

The price of middle class respectability is hard work, supervision,
anxiety, striving for status and authority, and passive consumerism.
People in this group do not have the opportunity to experience much
unselfconscious abandonment or excitement in their daily responsibilities.
The new churches are fulfilling the needs of such people by providing
them with immediate and gratifying experiences.

However, the consequences of conversion and membership of the new
churches revealed by this survey, we believe, have far-reaching implications for the situation in South Africa today.   The new churches
are not small eccentric sects getting on with their business in dingy,
derelict halls.   They are attracting enormous numbers of converts
ranging from film stars to politicians, sportspeople and ordinary
people in all the major cities of South Africa.   The popular media,
although often critical of the new churches, has tended to concentrate
on their more sensational aspects: healing, glossolalia, being slain
in the spirit, and cash flowing.   The number of articles appearing
in newspapers and magazines reflects the interest and concern evoked
by the new churches.   Almost everyone has something to say about the
born-again movement in general and the new churches in particular.

For this reason certain features of the new churches revealed in this
study should be examined and viewed with extreme caution.

Authoritarianism and anti-intellectualism

Historically, fundamentalist churches have opposed intellectualism.
What is of concern is that the anti-intellectualism of the new
churches appears to preclude almost all critical thinking.   They
provide formulae for living, for getting wealthy, healthy and happy,
for ensuring a secure and unthreatened future in this country, for

dealing with poverty and suffering and psychological problems. The
new churches seem to have a formula for everything and anything.

Rational thinking, doubt and uncertainty are regarded either as
demonic, or as avenues for Satan to penetrate human defences. Very
little information apart from that which confirms the belief system
of new church members is allowed to penetrate the discourse of the
congregation. Most of the spare time of new church charismatic
adherents is spent in church activities and most of their friends
are also new church members. They tend to avoid going to the cinema
and they tend to read only that which directly confirms their beliefs.
This serves to encourage commitment but also closed-mindedness,
fanaticism and inability to consider other points of view. This
attitude bodes badly for dialogue between churches or for attempts
at ecumenicity.

Conway and Siegelman (1981) speak of a phenomenon called 'snapping'.
Based on their study in the United States of America of the pro-
liferation of cults, mass therapies and evangelical movements which
promise and effect drastic alterations in personality, they have
identified a particular 'snapping' moment on conversion. Snapping
heralds not merely an alteration of behaviour and belief - it can
bring about a much deeper and more comprehensive change in individual
awareness and personality. Conway and Siegelman (1981) believe that
the intense experience of snapping may affect fundamental information-
processing capacities of the brain, which they believe leads to an
information processing disease.

> "In all the world there is nothing quite so inpenetrable
> as a human mind snapped shut with bliss. No call to
> reason, no emotional appeal can get through its armour
> of self-proclaimed joy." (Conway and Siegelman 1981,
> p. 62.)

Although Conway and Siegelman (1981) do not condemn evangelical movements out of hand and have immense respect for many born-again believers,
they have strong reservations about movements which encourage their
members to put their minds 'on hold' by stopping all self-reflection,

and criticism of the movement itself. We suggest that the new churches
are encouraging their members to put their minds on hold by telling them
that Satan is ever-present and trying to make them doubt their faith.
Their literal interpretation of the Bible is encouraging people to
accept anything so long as it has a Biblical verse to support it. In
telling people to cast down all vain reasonings and bring every thought
into the captivity of the obedience of Christ they could be encouraging
mindless passivity instead of mature, critical and responsible faith.
The faith teachings tend to deny negative realities. This attitude
encourages massive, ultimately destructive, psychological repression.
Interviewers noted the uniformity of responses of new church charismatics - the same Biblical verses, the same litanies of happiness
were repeatedly heard, to the extent that identical language and
answers were given by different respondents, at different times, in
different places. This is not to suggest that the respondents were
insincere but rather that they are being encouraged to think of their
lives in terms of 'pat' and snappy answers.

Instant gratification

Consumer capitalism and Christianity have never been easy bedfellows.
Traditionally Christianity has drawn attention to the poor and pointed
out the responsibilities of Christians in relation to their poorer
brethren. We suggest that the situation in South Africa makes
Christians in general uncomfortable. It is difficult to feel
satisfied and enjoy privileges when others are suffering.

It appears that the new churches, by sanctioning and exalting wealth
and success now, and concomitantly denigrating the poor as living
out of God's favour, are tailor-made to suit the needs of guilty
consumers. The late Professor Verryn of UNISA referred to this
as "sprinkling holy water on capitalism".

Magliato (1981), commenting on the faith/prosperity churches in America,
says that the American obsession with success, shortcuts and pleasure
has created this Americanised gospel which offers a shortcut to the

American dream. We suggest that the middle class South African dream
is very similar to the American one. The attractive 'instant package,
name it claim it' gospel of the new churches panders to the desire for
instant gratification, as well as assuring members that the pressing
problems of a rapidly changing industrial society torn with racism
will be solved,not by massive social change,but by the miracle of
everyone being born-again and retaining or increasing their wealth
and privilege.

The desire for instant consumer gratification is also satisfied by
the style of the new churches. Miracles are now, signs and wonders
are now, 'if you haven't got tongues you'll get tongues'. The old
Christian ethic of delayed gratification to encourage a healthy
appreciation of God's mercy and generosity has been turned upside
down. Many would say this is a good thing - people need fulfilment
in this life, not only a pie in the sky promise which may never come
to fruition. However there is a fine line between self-fulfilment
now, and a blithe disregard for one's fellow human beings and the
real causes of suffering and inequality, which are not Satanic but
rooted in the unjust structures of this society.

Membership trends indicate that the new churches have not been successful amongst working class African people. We suggest that this is
due to the very nature of the prosperity message, critically condemned
in the following quote:

> "Let those who teach that all the redeemed ought to be wealthy
> and have wealth go to Bangladesh and Cambodia with their
> teaching on prosperity. Let them preach their Wall
> Street gospel to the poverty-stricken masses and tell
> them to claim abundance and material goods. Any gospel
> that does not work equally well in the Congo or in Chicago
> is not the New Testament gospel." (Magliato 1981, p.21.)

It appears that the new church movement will not become a major force
amongst the majority of South Africa's people because structural injustices and inequalities need stronger remedies than simply preaching
the prosperity message and hoping that the hearts of the leaders in
the government will be softened by being born-again. Its appeal will

be limited to aspirant or new middle class people who are
materially relatively advantaged but perceive themselves as being
relatively deprived.

Political involvement

The new churches' claims to be apolitical are not substantiated by
the results of this survey.   Their aversion to the social gospel
is not neutral and amounts to support of the status quo.   When
new church pastors were asked whether there were any laws which
they or their churches would regard as unjust the strongest
criticism was of petty apartheid.   When asked about specific laws
concerning group areas, mixed marriages and removals not one new
church pastor said that these were unjust.   They supported such
laws by saying that there were sound reasons for their existence.
Despite new church charismatic respondents' persistent claims that
they were not interested in politics and that the church should not
'involve itself with politics' their attitudes and voting preferences
revealed a consistent pro-government position.

9.3   ASSESSMENT OF AND IMPLICATIONS FOR THE MAINLINE CHURCHES

Our results have shown that mainline church traditional respondents
are generally only somewhat satisfied with their churches.   They
criticise their churches for being too concerned with tradition, for
being dry and boring and for lacking genuine fellowship.   They dis-
like what they perceive as being too much political involvement.
The mainline churches cannot simply rely on denominational loyalty
to ensure that their members will not 'defect' to the new churches.
The chief criticisms of new churches made by mainline church
traditional respondents were that they were too emotional, hysterical
or exuberant, i.e. the criticisms concerned the charismatic features
of the new churches.   Once a person has been born-again these
reservations about emotionalism disappear.   Indeed many of the new
church charismatic respondents reported that they had, prior to
being 'saved', been extremely reserved.

Many mainline Christians (and all the new church charismatics) feel
that the hierarchy, tradition and authority structures of the established denominations are outmoded and out-dated.   They point to what
they refer to as meaningless and irrelevant sermons, inaccessible
clergy, tedious services and unenthusiastic congregations in the
established churches.   Contrast this with the very 'normal' experience
of going along to the Embassy Cinema on a Sunday evening, seeing things
happen, getting slain in the spirit, and hearing familiar modern jargon,
contemporary music and a message that is quite unthreatening and
unchallenging, although apparently relevant.

The conclusion to be drawn from these feelings is not that the mainline churches should compete with the new churches in trying to be
more 'with-it'.   Rather, the feelings reflect dissatisfaction with
perceived lack of participation in the decisions taken by and af-
fecting the mainline churches.   More mainline church members, not
only the church council and elders must be given scope for participating
in the decisions of their church, and the scope of such participation
must be wider.   They must have knowledge of the church decisions, of
the method in which such decisions are taken, and they must be able to
influence those decisions.   It is suggested that real participation in
the affairs and decisions of the church are a substantive and desirable
alternative to the illusory forms of participation that obtain in
the new churches.   Certainly, the criticism of formality and tradition
levelled against the mainline churches may be somewhat dispelled.

In order to meet the needs of their members while at the same time
countering the appeal of the new churches we suggest that the established
churches need to take the following factors into consideration:

Commitment

Kelley's (1977) hypothesis concerning the growth of conservative
churches is supported by the findings of this study.   The more of
certain demands that are made on people, the more committed they
tend to become.   It appears that people do not necessarily recoil

from demands but rather respond positively. The results show that
the more people participate in church-related activities, the more
committed they become to their church.

This is not to suggest that the mainline churches should assume the
authoritarian features of the new churches or exploit the authoritarian tendencies of their members.

Commitment is likely to be generated if members of the church are
given real avenues for involvement in church activities. There
are many forms of participation besides those fostered by the new
churches: forms that are more compassionate, merciful and generous.

It is possible to obtain commitment from people once their needs for
genuine fellowship and joyful worship, for relevant teachings and
adequate explanations for perplexing issues, are satisfied. The
new churches make much use of small, informal home-fellowship groups.
They seem to play a very important role in facilitating and fostering
participation and commitment among church members. They provide a
forum for easy and frank discussion of issues that may have been
perturbing. The mainline churches could make good use of the
home-fellowship context. The small meetings promote genuine dis-
cursive involvement in church activities and doctrine and can be
successfully used to share and discuss personal problems (one of
their functions for the new church adherents).

The social gospel

Our results have shown that many people are resistant to the social
gospel, particularly disliking being told what to do from the pulpit.
The churches in South Africa face an enormous challenge of goodwill
in motivating their members to work for a better society. The
preaching of a social gospel often results in white people simply
feeling guilty, uncomfortable, doubtful and resentful. By contrast
the new churches sidestep the issue of social justice completely by
offering a comfortable, comforting, 'punchy' experience which makes

no demands on members to exercise their Christian responsibility in combatting unjust social structures.

Many new church charismatics had felt, while still members of the mainline churches, guilty and unjustly accused for their relative privileges and advantages in South African society.   The new churches generate none of these feelings.   On the contrary they encourage people to renounce feelings of doubt, guilt and uncertainty as being engendered by Satan.   The pursuit of self-fulfilment in all its forms - spiritual, physical and financial, is explained as being the desire of God.   If people do not prosper it is taken to be their own and Satan's fault and no cause for active intervention by other Christians.   In the words of Ray McCauley, the head of Rhema Bible Church, on the recent television programme presented by SATV, *"Be concerned about yourself rather than with everyone else around you. If you have Jesus he will take care of others as he sees fit."*

Perhaps the lesson for the mainline churches is that privilege brings with it certain alienations and distortions for the people ostensibly benefitting from that privilege.   Its impact on them is usually more subtle than its obvious effects on the unprivileged or oppressed people.   The relatively privileged people in South Africa need to be shown the distortions and burdens which they carry for their privileges principally: the abandonment of control over the factors that affect their lives to the government which maintains the privileges, and the conservative limitations which a system of this nature necessarily places over their personal lives (fear of neighbours, fear of losing property, fear of the poor).   The relatively advantaged people of this country should not be blamed and made to feel guilty for the injustices.   They too are its victims as the new churches are telling them in a massively simplistic and illusory way.

A reasonable compassionate type of Christianity can be encouraged by the established churches through discussion of a system that distorts the lives of all South Africans.

Insecurity in South Africa today

Several references have been made to the general uncertainty in the lives
of white South Africans today, and some evidence of this is forthcoming
in various aspects of the results of this study. Some of this insecurity
obviously is a manifestation of universal anxiety about the future
present in any population, but a great deal of it is specifically a
South African problem —— the knowledge among most whites that sooner
or later substantial changes have to occur in our society. Economic and
political insecurity is normally associated with a conservative mood.
The responses of European and American populations, including students,
to unemployment and inflation in recent times have borne this out. There
is no doubt that very dramatic swings in the attitudes of the white
population are possible if this insecurity were to become augmented.
Some would anticipate change by becoming more liberal in orientation
but most would react by becoming more conservative and resistant.

The new church charismatics have "resolved" their fears, albeit in what
must be an unconstructive way. In a sense they have put themselves beyond
the reach of most organised religion and there is little that the
established churches can do. What of the non-charismatics, however,
many of whom are still attempting to come to terms with current anxieties
in more rational ways? This study did not focus on them and yet their
problems are of greater salience to the established churches. The
results in Table 2, for the very small sample of everyday churchgoers
are very disquieting in their implications.

One important conclusion of this study must be that those anxieties dare
not be neglected by the church, and the flight of the new church
charismatics is a telling pointer to the possible consequences of such
neglect. Unfortunately the ways in which such fears and anxieties
interact with religious experience in the established churches are
largely unknown and this study could not provide more than scraps of
insight.

It is perhaps necessary that a further study be undertaken, this time
concentrating on the established churchgoer, the occasional churchgoer
and the non-churchgoer in order to explore the impact on religious

life of current fears and worries. Even without specific insights from
such a study, however, a few tentative comments on the church's role
may be useful.

A church of social justice in our situation must attempt to strike a
balance between moral injunctions on whites to change and to forego
racial privileges, and support and reassurance in the process of that
change. Yet the typical established churchgoer is too secularised and
rational to accept unquestioning faith as sufficient support in the
process of change. This churchgoer, however, is also not sufficiently
well-informed to be able to contemplate the processess of political
conflict and change with academic or scientific equanimity. Hence
the established churchgoer can easily come to exist in a state of
ambivalence; with his or her sentiments a mixture of guilt, fear and
resistance.

Faced with this understandable failure of courage among so many committed
white Christians the established church is presented with the formidable
task of building or rebuilding the confidence and sense of basic
security which is a pre-condition of openness to change. As we understand it such a task can be pursued inter alia along three lines, which
are not mutually exclusive but probably complimentary.

The first is the development of faith, perhaps not only as a trust in
divine Providence but also as a trust in the power of collective
Christian commitment and organisation to influence the future course of
events in order to protect whites from possible victimisation and
oppression. One important element in the belief structure of the new
churches, as we have seen, is a sense of power in faith. A similar
sense of power in faith, but less selfishly and materially and more
rationally directed, is perhaps desirable in established Christianity
as well.

A second element is knowledge. For example, most careful analyses suggest
that whites would be more secure in a changing South Africa than they
think. Political change, no matter how swift, is very unlikely in the
longer run to substantially weaken the enormous value of the skills

and experience of whites in our complex economy and administration.
Whites in South Africa have simply too large a contribution to make
to the welfare of the whole population for them to be relegated to
the role of a dispossessed and marginal minority. Just as whites must
come to terms with black aspirations so any hypothetical black
government, for example, will have to recognise the enormous bargain-
ing power which whites will continue to exercise by virture of skills,
experience and potential solidarity. In this sense, South Africa,
with well over four million whites has a completely different structure
to, say Zimbabwe for example, where whites were fewer than 300 000
in number.

Other compelling arguments can also be advanced which imply less insecurity
for whites under conditions of change than most whites recognise. Even
today,.when most black groups share common goals of opposing the policies
of separation and segregation, black people are by no means united.
In a more open society there will always be substantial black political
interests consonant with those of non-black minorities. Another fact,
for example, is that South Africa is a much more differentiated and
complex society than any black state to the North where authoritarian,
single party domination has emerged.

We would suggest that the church, in dealing with political issues as it
must, in addition to its moral prophecy, needs to equip its adherents
with a more sophisticated approach to understanding the possible futures
than is currently the case.

The third element is much more elusive and problematic, but ties in closely
with the first. It concerns the issue of "identity" in a very basic
sense. It is probably true to say that where excessive materialism,
status concern and concern with in-group ethnic identity exist among
communities they are to a considerable extent symptoms of uncertain
concepts of self in the individuals who make up those communities and
societies. The problem, needless to say, is in no way peculiar to
South Africa.

We are aware that one of the major basic themes in Christianity
has been the issue of personal identity, and perhaps a central role
in ministry is to assist individuals in deepening their own sense of
role, purpose and personality without reliance on the more external
trappings of status, wealth and group membership. We are also aware,
naturally, that this calling of the church is among its most complex
of challenges. Very often organised religion, often unintentionally
perhaps, has addressed the problem of identity most effectively by
providing an alternative in-group identification —— that of the
denomination or sect. This does little more than shift the problem from
one social sphere to another.

Very tentatively, because we are obviously lacking in the theological
insights to fully grasp the ramifications of the issue, the church in
South Africa has perhaps a more urgent calling to address these
problems of identity than many other parts of the world. The church
has what one may refer to as a "group therapeutic" role in attempting
to work even harder than it does to try to help individuals to enjoy
a sense of worth without external social props or privileges which
signal social superiority.

These elements are mentioned simply as possibilities for debate in the
church regarding the development of its role and ministry. We have not
attempted to specify our suggestions in any detail since specific
approaches can only be adequately developed by the churches themselves.
We would simply like to emphasise once again the urgency of the problem.
Our small sample of churchgoers in the established churches is probably
not a balanced representation of white Christians, since we have noted
that they appear to be more "liberal" than average. We would suggest
that the degree of confusion in the established church movement in
general is probably greater than our provisional results suggest.

Relationship with the new churches

The late Trevor Verryn, in conversation with the authors, pointed out that many members of the established church clergy are impressed by the growth and flashy secular signs of success of the new churches. They feel inadequate, insecure and consequently hesitant about criticising the new churches because they themselves are not ostensibly successful and because it is considered unChristian to condemn other Christians.

The new churches have little hesitation in ridiculing or adopting a patronising attitude towards churches which they consider are not moving with God. Established church clergy can, and indeed should, without sensationalism or exaggeration, point out the dangers inherent in the new churches, and expose the hostility of the new churches to much that is correctly and essentially Christian, particularly humility, meekness and selfless devotion to one's fellow man.

The new churches' belief that doubt, uncertainty, psychological problems and critical thinking are due to Satan's influence, needs to be shown to be inherently authoritarian and contrary to a fully human existence. The alarming submissiveness and abandonment of rationality by new church charismatic adherents is epitomised by the following statement of a new church charismatic respondent who felt uncomfortable answering the questions put to her:

- *The trouble is it's getting me thinking - it's confusing.*

Such abandonment of rationality should be combatted by more active intellectual and practical participation in church activities.

In Christian terms, the doctrinal foundation of the new churches can be shown to be incorrect, if not heretical. The fundamentally manipulative attitude towards God, embodied in the prosperity message, can be shown to be contrary to the very basis of Christian faith. In the words of Magliato (1981, p.144), "Jesus is Lord. I cannot make him my servant."

APPENDIX 1:

ADDITIONAL TABLES

TABLE 45:   CHURCH INVOLVEMENT PRIOR TO JOINING PRESENT DENOMINATION

Percentage of respondents in each sample group who had actively
belonged to another denomination:

	NCC %	ECC %	MCT %
Immediately before	80	30	30
Before but with a gap of some years	10	20	3
Before but only as a child	10	20	7
Still same church	0	30	60
	n = 30	n = 20	n = 30

NCC = New church charismatics
ECC = Established church charismatics
MCT = Mainline church traditionalists

TABLE 46:   CHANGES IN DEGREE OF PARTICIPATION IN PRESENT
            DENOMINATION

Percentage of respondents in each sample group whose participation
had changed in the following ways:

	NCC %	ECC %	MCT %
Active — More active - before active	20	30	20
Consistently active	80	15	30
More active - before inactive	0	40	7
Inactive — Less active but still active	0	10	7
Inactive - before active	0	5	27
Never active	0	0	10
	n = 30	n = 20	n = 30

NCC = New church charismatics
ECC = Established church charismatics
MCT = Mainline church traditionalists

TABLE 47: REASONS FOR INCREASED PARTICIPATION IN THE CHURCH

Percentage of respondents in each sample group who gave the
following reasons for increased participation:

	NCC	ECC	MCT
	%*	%*	%*
No increase in participation	80	30	77
Gradual development/spiritual growth	17	5	0
Joining sub-group, given leadership position, active during services	7	30	20
Personal crisis - illness, army, death	0	20	0
For the sake of the family	0	5	7
Because of being born-again	0	50	0
Other reasons	3	20	0
	n = 30	n = 20	n = 30

NCC = New church charismatics
ECC = Established church charismatics
MCT = Mainline church traditionalists
* Respondents could give more than one reason

TABLE 48: REASONS FOR DECREASED PARTICIPATION

Percentage of respondents in each sample group who gave the
following reasons for decreased participation:

	NCC	ECC	MCT
	%*	%*	%*
No decrease in participation	100	80	57
Pressure of work - need to rest - too old	-	5	17
More important/better things to do	-	0	17
Too busy with family/spouse not a churchgoer	-	15	13
Disenchanted with church - lack of fellowship	-	0	10
Other reasons	-	5	13
	n = 30	n = 20	n = 30

NCC = New church charismatics
ECC = Established church charismatics
MCT = Mainline church traditionalists
* Respondents could give more than one reason

TABLE 49:   CONSCIOUS SEARCH FOR SUITABLE CHURCH

Percentage of respondents in each sample group who stated that
they had been consciously searching for an appropriate church:

	NCC	ECC	MCT
	%	%	%
	57	33	17

n = 30 n = 20 n = 30

NCC = New church charismatics
ECC = Established church charismatics
MCT = Mainline church traditionalists

TABLE 50:   INVOLVEMENT IN NON-CHURCH ORGANISATIONS

Percentage of respondents in each sample group who belonged to the
following organisations and clubs:

	NCC		ECC		MCT	
	%* 5 yrs ago	%* Now	%* 5 yrs ago	%* Now	%* 5 yrs ago	%* Now
No other organisations	40	50	40	45	43	27
Welfare organisations	10	0	25	20	10	13
Work-related organisations	3	13	10	20	7	7
Sports clubs	34	23	20	20	30	40
Social clubs	17	20	15	20	17	13
Hobby clubs	13	7	15	0	13	17
Political organisations	0	0	0	0	0	10
Other organisations	13	3	5	5	3	0

n = 30   n = 20   n = 30

NCC = New church charismatics
ECC = Established church charismatics
MCT = Mainline church traditionalists

* Respondents could give more than one response

TABLE 51: BREAKDOWN OF CHURCH MEMBERSHIP

Percentage of respondents in each sample group who belonged to
the following denominations:

	NCC %	ECC %	MCT %	Total %
Christian Centre	100	0	0	37,5
Roman Catholic	0	10	27	12,5
Anglican	0	20	33	17,5
Methodist	0	30	20	15,0
Presbyterian	0	5	20	8,5
Full Gospel	0	35	0	9,0

n = 30 n = 20 n = 30

NCC = New church charismatics
ECC = Established church charismatics
MCT = Mainline church traditionalists

TABLE 52: LENGTH OF TIME AS BORN-AGAIN CHRISTIAN

Percentage of respondents in the charismatic sample
who had been born-again for the following number of
years:

	NCC %	ECC %
0 - 2 years	30	21
3 - 5 years	30	42
6 - 20 years	40	37

n = 30 n = 20

NCC = New church charismatics
ECC = Established church charismatics

TABLE 53: LENGTH OF TIME IN PRESENT CHURCH/DENOMINATION

Percentage of respondents in each sample group who had
belonged to their particular denomination for the following
number of years:

	NCC %	ECC %	MCT %
Always the same	0	30	60
0 - 2	53	30	3
3 - 5 years	43	15	10
6+ years	4	25	27

n = 30 n = 20 n = 30

NCC = New church charismatics
ECC = Established church charismatics
MCT = Mainline church traditionalists

TABLE 54: SEX

	Total %	NCC %	ECC %	MCT %
Male	49	50	50	47
Female	51	50	50	53

n = 30 n = 20 n = 30

NCC = New church charismatics
ECC = Established church charismatics
MCT = Mainline church traditionalists

TABLE 55: AGE

	Total %	NCC %	ECC %	MCT %
19 - 29	25	20	35	23
30 - 39	26	30	20	27
40 - 49	19	27	15	14
50 - 59	21	20	5	33
60+	9	3	25	3
		n = 30	n = 20	n = 30

NCC = New church charismatics
ECC = Established church charismatics
MCT = Mainline church traditionalists

TABLE 56: MARITAL STATUS

	Total %	NCC %	ECC %	MCT %
Single	20	20	25	17
Married	67	60	70	73
Widowed	3	0	5	3
Divorced	10	20	0	7
		n = 30	n = 20	n = 30

NCC = New church charismatics
ECC = Established church charismatics
MCT = Mainline church traditionalists

TABLE 57: EDUCATION

	Total %	NCC %	ECC %	MCT %
Below Std. 10	26	30	35	17
Std. 10	31	37	20	33
Std. 10 plus diploma	23	30	10	23
Std. 10 plus degree	20	3	35	27
		n = 30	n = 20	n = 30

NCC = New church charismatics
ECC = Established church charistmatics
MCT = Mainline church traditionalists

TABLE 58: OCCUPATION

	Total %	NCC %	ECC %	MCT %
Professional/Semi-Professional	14	3	15	23
Managerial/Executive	11	3	15	17
People operating for individual profit or commission	18	30	10	10
Clerical/Secretarial	15	17	10	17
Artisan and other blue collar	5	7	0	7
Retired and other	5	7	10	0
Housewife	20	23	25	13
Student	12	10	15	13
		n = 30	n = 20	n = 30

NCC = New church charistmatics
ECC = Established church charismatics
MCT = Mainline church traditionalists

196.

TABLE 59: MONTHLY INCOME				
	Total	NCC	ECC	MCT
	%	%	%	%
R0 - R500	26	30	39	17
R500 - 999	19	11	17	27
R1 000 - 1 499	28	30	22	30
R1 500 - 1 999	15	22	11	10
R2 000 - 2 499	8	7	6	10
R2 500 - 2 999	1	0	5	6
R3 000+	3	0	0	0
Mean		R1 150	R823	R1 100
		n = 30	n = 20	n = 30

NCC = New church charismatics
ECC = Established church charismatics
MCT = Mainline church traditionalists

APPENDIX 2:

GLOSSARY

APPENDIX 2:   GLOSSARY

(World Christian Encyclopaedia, David B. Barrett (Ed.), was used as a basis for this glossary.)

Baptism of the Holy Spirit — generally means receiving the out-pouring or infilling by the Holy Spirit but is, in the new churches, synonomous with the gift of tongues which is one of the signs of being infilled with the Holy Spirit.

Born-again Christians — those who have had, or claim to have had an experience of new birth in Christ.

Charismatic revival/renewal — the pentecostal or neo-pentecostal renewal or revival movement character-ised by healings, tongues, prophesyings, et al.   (See Gifts of the Holy Spirit.)

Ecumenical movement — the movement to bring together all denominations and Christian bodies, for fellowship, consultation, joint action and eventually organic union.

Evangelical — characterised by commitment to personal religion (including new birth or personal conversion experience), reliance on Holy Scripture as the only basis for faith and Christian living, emphasis on preaching and evangelism, and usually on conservatism in theology.

Evangelism — the activities involved in spreading the gospel: zealous preaching of the gospel, commonly applied to persons or religious bodies that are dedicated to converting people to Christ - outspoken proclamation of the Christian message.

Fundamentalism — a conservative movement in Protestantism originating in opposition to modernist tendencies and emphasising as fundamental to Christianity a group of 5 or 7 basic doctrines: inerrant verbal inspiration of the Bible, Virgin Birth, miracles of Christ, Resurrection, total depravity of man, substitutionary atonement, premillenial Second Coming.

Gifts of the Holy Spirit (charisms) — gifts of grace conferred directly for the good of others: instantaneous sanctification - the ability to prophesy, practice divine healing, speak in tongues (glossolalia), interpret tongues, discern true spirits from false ones et al.

Glossolalia — the gift of tongues; ecstatic speech usually unintelligible to hearers.

Infilling of the Holy Spirit — see baptism of the Holy Spirit.

Pentecostalism — A Christian confession or ecclesiastical tradition holding the distinctive teaching that all Christians should seek a post-conversion experience called the Baptism with/of the Holy Spirit, and that a Spirit-baptised believer may receive one or more of the supernatural gifts of the Holy Spirit.

Slain in the spirit   - a term used by the new churches to indicate falling down under the power of the Holy Spirit.

Spirit-filled   - see baptism of the Holy Spirit.

APPENDIX 3:

QUESTIONNAIRE

1. What church do you belong to?

   ----

2. How often do you attend services at _____?

More than once a week	Once a week	Once a fortnight	Once a month	Twice a year	Less than once a year	Never

3. a)i. For how long have you been an active member of your present church?

   ----

   ii. Have you always been as active as you are now? (PROBE)

   ----

   iii. What has made you more active/less active?

   ----

or b) i. For how long have you not really been an active member of your present church?

   ----

   ii. Could you tell me why you are no longer/have never been active in the _____ church?

   ----

4. a) Do you consider yourself to be a born-again Christian?

   ----

   b) When did you become a born-again Christian?

   ----

4. c)   Were you brought up in the _____ church?

If not, when did you join/become a _____

(PROBE FOR CHURCH ATTENDANCE HISTORY AND MOTIVATION)

---

5. *   How did you come to know about the _____?

---

6. *   What encouraged you to join the _____?

---

7.   Did you belong to any other church before this one?

Which one? _____

8.   (If yes)   Why did you leave the church to which you
previously belonged?

---

9. The church has certain tasks to perform. Some are very
    important, others less so. I will read you some of the
    tasks of a church. For each one I want you to tell me
    whether it is: of great importance/fairly important/
    unimportant/ nothing to do with the church.

	Great	Fair	Unimportant	Not Church
- helping people overcome fear and anxiety	-----	----	-----------	------
- winning people to Christ	-----	----	-----------	------
- helping the needy	-----	----	-----------	------
- teaching meekness and humility	-----	----	-----------	------
- actively working for political and social justice for all	-----	----	-----------	------
- ministering to and helping people with their problems	-----	----	-----------	------
- teaching the need for self-discipline, hard work and duty	-----	----	-----------	-------
- giving clear answers in this complex modern world	-----	----	-----------	-------
- working for the equality of all people	-----	----	-----------	-------
- giving Bible instruction	-----	----	-----------	-------
- giving inspiration and joy in worship	-----	----	-----------	-------
- helping people to succeed and prosper	-----	----	-----------	-------
- providing fellowship and a sense of belonging	-----	----	-----------	-------
- preserving traditional forms of worship	-----	----	-----------	-------
- getting back to simple Bible truths	-----	----	-----------	-------
- providing freedom of worship	-----	----	-----------	-------
- teaching the congregations about the injustices in this country	------	----	-----------	------
- providing signs and wonders and miracles	------	----	-----------	-------
- urging the government to abandon apartheid as unChristian	------	----	-----------	-------

10. How satisfied are you with the church to which you belong?

Completely satisfied	Somewhat satisfied	Uncertain	Somewhat dissatisfied	Completely dissatisfied
---------	---------	---------	------------	------------

a) (If NOT completely satisfied) Why are you not completely satisfied?

    _____

    _____

    _____

b) (If completely satisfied) What makes you completely satisfied?

    _____

    _____

    _____

11. Do you have any criticisms of the denominational mainline churches in general?

    _____

    _____

    _____

    _____

12a.
* What have you found at the Christian Centre that you did not find in the _____?

    _____

    _____

    _____

    _____

or 12b. Do you ever feel that you might want to join one of the newer non-denominational churches? Probe.

    _____

    _____

    _____

13. In your view, Christian <u>individuals</u>, because they are Christians, should:

	I AGREE	I DISAGREE	I AM NOT SURE
a. Live a life of devoted prayer, Bible study and worshop	------	-------	--------
b. Be active in proclaiming the Gospel to other individuals	------	-------	--------
c. Be involved in community welfare projects for the less privileged	------	------	--------
d. Work for racial harmony and reconciliation between individuals	------	------	--------
e. Actively work for social justice	------	------	--------
f. Be a community of persons who know and care for one another	------	------	--------
g. Be mainly concerned for the needs of their own individual parish	------	------	--------
h. Be mainly concerned with the most urgent social, political and economic problems of society	------	-------	-------
i. Other (specify)_____	------	-------	--------

14. In the past 5 years /before you were born-again which of the following problems seriously applied to you?

	Yes	Somewhat	No
- illness	---	----------	---
- financial problems	---	----------	---
- marital problems	---	----------	---
- death of a close relative or friend	---	----------	---
- alcohol problems	---	----------	---
- demonic problems/occult involvement	---	----------	---
- depression	---	----------	---
- anxiety/worry	---	----------	---
- about job			
- about future	---	----------	---
- about maintaining a decent standard of living	---	----------	---
- any other _____	---	----------	---

15. Could you tell me which of these problems apply to you at present?

----

16. Could you tell me how you feel about yourself now compared with how you felt about yourself before you were born again/ five years ago? (PROBE)

----

17. Has being born-again changed your social life?/Has your social life changed during the last 5 years? (PROBE)

----

18. Has being born-again changed your attitudes to the political situation in South Africa?/Have your political attitudes changed during the last 5 years? (PROBE)

----

19. Apart from attending services, what other church activities are you involved in?

    ----

20. How often do you read the Bible?

More than once a day	Once a day	Once a week	Occasionally	Never
---------	------	------	-------------	-----

21. Do you read any other religious literature regularly? (PROBE)

    ----

22. Apart from the Bible and religious works do you read any of the following regularly?

Newspapers	Magazines	Novels	Non-fiction
----------	---------	-------	-------------

    Specify: _____

    ----

23. How much money do you donate to thechurch per month?

Nothing	R5	R5-20	R20-50	R50-100	R100-150	R150-200	R200-500
-------	---	-----	------	-------	--------	---------	--------

24. Have you ever had the feeling that God has performed a miracle in your life?

Could you give me some of the most outstanding examples?

----

25. Has the presence of God or the Holy Spirit ever physically affected you?

Could you tell me about some of the most dramatic examples of this?

----

26. Is is possible to have a good relationship with God without attending church?   Yes_____   No _____

If YES, how is this possible?   If NO, why not ?_____

SECTION B

CHRISTIAN BELIEFS

I am going to read you some statements concerning Christian beliefs.
After each one I want you to say whether you agree/disagree or whether
you are uncertain.

		AGREE	UNCERTAIN	DISAGREE
27.	I believe that all of the Bible is inspired by God and is <u>literally</u> true.	-----	---------	---------
28.	There is no such thing as a physical hell where men are punished after death for their sins.	----	---------	--------
29.	I believe there is a supernatural being, the devil, who continually tries to lead people into sin.	-----	---------	---------
30.	It is a great relief to have handed over all my decisions and worries to the Lord.	-----	---------	--------
31.	A child is <u>not</u> born into the world already guilty of sin.	-----	---------	--------
32.	In the world today, people like me can be persecuted for religious beliefs.	-----	---------	--------
33.	God wants us to be financially prosperous.	-----	---------	--------
34.	Eternal life is not only for born-again Christians.	-----	---------	--------
35.	We should be generous in giving because he who casts his bread upon the waters shall have it returned ten-fold.	-----	---------	---------
36	A practising religious Hindu could gain eternal life.	-----	---------	---------
37.	We should submit to those placed in authority over us without question.	-----	---------	---------
	a) wives to husbands.	------	---------	---------
	b) citizens to government.	------	---------	---------
38.	Apartheid is a sin.	----	---------	---------
39.	There is nothing bad or ungodly about being financially prosperous.	----	---------	---------
40.	I am not sure that I have found the meaning and purpose of life.	-----	---------	---------
41.	It is the devil who plants doubt and uncertainty in peoples' minds.	-----	---------	---------

42. One sees innocent people suffering every day.   What does this mean?

    a.   It is part of God's plan   ---------

    b.   It is the work of the devil   ---------

    c.   It sometimes makes me wonder whether there is a God   ---------

    d.   I don't understand but I am sure God does not want people to suffer   ---------

SECTION C   GENERAL ATTITUDES

I am going to read a series of statements to you covering a wide
variety of topics. There are no right or wrong answers. Just
give your opinion by saying whether you:

Strongly   Agree   Uncertain   Disagree   Strongly
agree   somewhat   _____   somewhat   disagree

	SA	A	U	D	SD
43. I enjoy watching TV.					
44. A few good strong leaders could make this country better than all the laws and talk					
45. Large incomes should be taxed much more than they are now, so that everyone can share in the wealth of this land.					
46. Newspapers exaggerate the condition of blacks in this country.					
47. It is difficult for me to take orders and do what I am told.					
48. Unfortunately it seems that now that blacks have taken over Zimbabwe has much less chance of making progress.					
49. Most people can be trusted.					
50. In the past I certainly had more than my fair share of things to worry about.					
51. Conscientious objectors are traitors to their country.					
52. The incomes of most people are a fair measure of their contribution to the world.					
53. We should be willing to fight for our country without question.					

	SA	A	U	D	SD

54. All forms of racial discrimination should be made illegal.

55. These days a person does not really know who he can count on.

56. Maintenance of law and order in this country is more important than freedom for all.

57. It would be acceptable to me to have a coloured foreman supervising whites.

58. This world is run by the few people in power and there is not much the ordinary person can do about it.

59. Obedience and respect for authority are the most important virtues that children should learn.

60. It is better to take a chance on being a failure than to let your life get into a rut.

61. I think mixed marriages (between races) should be strongly discouraged.

62. The sexual orgies of the old Greeks and Romans are nursery school stuff compared to some of the goings on in the world today.

63. It is essential to vote when there is a general election.

64. Today everything in the world is unstable - we should be prepared for constant change, conflict and upheaval.

65. Detention without trial should be abolished in this country.

	SA	A	U	D	SD
66. I often find myself worrying about something or someone.					
67. Trade unions should become stronger and have more influence generally.					
68. On our own as individuals we cannot find direction and meaning in life.					
69. The only way to make sure that things get done right is to set up a definite and fixed schedule and never depart from it.					
70. The only way this country and the world will come right is through prayer and the spreading of the Gospel.					
71. I am really interested in the differences between the political parties					
72. If we all received equal salaries no-one would be motivated to do well.					
73. I have never felt better in my life than I do now.					
74. It is up to the government to make sure that everyone has a secure job and a good standard of living.					
75. I would willingly admit blacks to my church or club as personal friends.					
76. Many times I feel that I have little influence over the things that happen to me.					
77. National spectator sports like rugby, cricket and tennis are of no interest to me at all.					
78. In this complicated world of ours, the only way we can know what's going on is to rely on leaders or experts who can be trusted.					

SA   A   U   D   SD

79. One way or another all races and creeds should have the right to vote for our parliament.

80. If it is well-planned there is nothing wrong with black pupils being admitted to white schools

81. Poverty is mainly caused by weakness and lack of faith.

82. I like to fool around with new ideas even if they turn out later to be a total waste of time.

83. a) It is only natural for me to fear the the future in this country.
    b) It is only natural for most people to fear the future in this country.

84. When all is said and done, simple truths have more to offer than all the theories in science and education.

85. Success is mainly due to ability and hard work.

86. The general public is not qualified to vote on today's complex issues.

87. If neighbourhood standards did not drop, I would be quite happy to have African people living in my street as neighbours.

88. These days one is inclined to give up hope of amounting to something.

89. The world is a pretty dangerous place unless one has strong principles.

90. I am very confident of myself.

91. These days it is difficult to find real friends.

92. Once a person makes up his/her mind about something he/she should stick to his/her conclusion instead of repeatedly rehashing the question.

93. A sensible person should mind his/her own business and not concern him/herself about politics.

	SA	A	U	D	SD

94. There may be a few exceptions but in general Indians are pretty much alike.

95. Sometimes I feel that there is nothing a person like me can do which will make a difference.

SECTION D

96. Which of the following parties would you be most likely to vote for if an election were held in the near future?

Conservative	HNP	Nationalist	NRP	PFP	None
------------	----	-----------	----	---	------

97. How many personal friends do you have whom you feel you can really trust and turn to in time of need?

None	1	2	3	4	5	more than 5
----	--	--	--	--	--	------------

98. How do you feel about the number of friends you have?

Too few	Few but enough	About right	Too many
-------	--------------	-----------	--------

99. What is your age?

Under 20	20-29	30-39	40-49	50-59	60 and over
--------	-----	-----	-----	-----	-----------

100. Sex: Male   Female

            _____   _____

101. Marital status:

Single (never married)	Married	Widowed	Divorced
----------------------	-------	-------	--------

102. What is the highest formal educational level you have achieved?

Stds.   3-5   -------------------------------------

      6   -------------------------------------

      8   -------------------------------------

     10   -------------------------------------

Diploma/Certificate   -------------------------------

Bachelors Degree, Honours, LLB, etc.   ----------------

Masters Degree   -------------------------------------

Doctorate   ---

103. What is your occupation at present?

----

104. How satisfied are you with your present occupation?

Completely satisfied	Somewhat satisfied	Uncertain	Somewhat dissatisfied	Completely dissatisfied
----------	-------	--------	------------	------------

105. What was your occupation 5 years ago?

----

106. How many times have you changed jobs in the last 10 years?

----

107. What is your present <u>monthly</u> income?

Under R500	R500-749	R750-999	R1000-1499	R1500-1999
---------	--------	--------	----------	----------

R2000-2499	R2500-2999	R3000+
---------	----------	-------

108. How many times have you moved house in the last 10 years?

----

109. How many times have you moved from one town to another in the last 10 years?

----

110. What other organisations or clubs do you belong to at present?

----

111. Did you belong to any organisations before you were born again/ 5 years ago?

----

112. Think of your 5 best friends.
How many of them

    - belong to (same church) _____

    - are born again/committed Christians _____

Code: * New church charismatics only

APPENDIX 4 :

SOURCES OF QUESTIONNAIRE ITEMS

APPENDIX 4 : SOURCES OF QUESTIONNAIRE ITEMS

Questionnaire items for Sections B & C were taken from the following sources and in some cases modified:

Adorno, Theodore, Else Frenkel-Brunswick, Daniel J. Levinson and R. Nevitt Sanford:
> The Fascism (F) Scale

Brown, Daniel G., and Warner I. Lowe:
> Inventory of religious belief

Bogardus E.S. :   Social distance scale

Meresko, Robert, Mandel Rubin, Franklin C. Shontz and William R. Morrow:
> Scale to measure rigidity of attitudes

Rokeach, Milton, and Albert Eglash:
> Scale for measuring intellectual conviction versus dogmatic conviction

Rundquist, E.A., and R.F. Sletto:
> Minnesota survey of opinions

Rundquist, E.A., and R.F. Sletto:
> The economic conservatism scale

Rundquist, E.A., and R.F. Sletto:
> The morale scale

Sampson, Donald L., and Howard P. Smith :
> Worldmindedness scale

Taylor, Janet A.: The revised form of the manifest anxiety scale.

222.

APPENDIX 5 :

PROBABILITY SURVEY OF RELIGIOUS INTEREST AMONG NATAL WHITES

Market Research Africa

TECHNICAL DETAILS OF THE SURVEY

OBJECTIVES OF THE SURVEY

The Natal White Omnijet is a syndicated survey which covers a range of different product categories to be researched for several individual clients.

COVERAGE

The survey covered White adults in Natal aged 16 and over, living in cities towns and villages.

SAMPLE

An area-stratified probability sample of 500 households was drawn from the MRA dwelling unit census. This sample includes all cities and major towns and a representative selection of smaller towns and villages. The sample is divided into 250 males and 250 females. In each household the male or female to be interviewed was chosen using a random selection grid and 3 calls were made on each household before substitution.

METHOD

Personal at-home interviews were conducted in the respondent's home language, using a structured questionnaire, a copy of which is given as an Appendix to this Report.

NOTES ON THE SAMPLE

Participants in the Natal White Omnijet survey may select any sample they require for their purposes. This may be either males or females only or combined. The applicable sample combination used for this study is shown at the top of each table.

INTERVIEWING

All interviews were carried out by trained experienced interviewers working under the direction of regional supervisors and the Field Manager. 10% validation checks are carried out on the work of each interviewer.

MARGIN OF ERROR

The results of any sample survey are subject to a statistical margin of error, inherent in the size of the sample and the unanimity of response. The table given in Appendix 1 shows the margin of error for various sample sizes and response rates.

ANALYSIS

Results have been post-weighted to known population proportions. The weighting cells used were province, community, age and sex.

Analysis has been done in total and by specified demographic breakdowns. Percentages are based on weighted data.

FIELDWORK was done during the period ...... SEPTEMBER 1983 ......

▲ SHOW CARD C1

▲ TOON KAART C1

C1. Thinking of your religious life, could you say which
one of the following **best** describes your position now?

● Dink aan u godsdienstige lewe, sal u asseblief vir my sê
watter van die volgende u posisie die **beste** beskryf?

▲ JUST GIVE ME THE NUMBER

▲ GEE MY NET DIE NOMMER

1. ●	Not Religious Nie godsdienstig	73-Y
2. ●	Jewish Joods	-X
3. ●	Born again charismatic in older churches like Anglican, Roman Catholic, Methodist etc. Weergebore charamatiese christen in ouer kerke soos die Anglikaanse, Rooms Katolieke, Metodiste kerke, ens.	-0
4. ●	Born again christian in pentecostal church like Full Gospel, Assemblies of God etc. Weergebore christen in 'n Pinksterkerk soos die Volle Evangelie, "Assemblies of God", ens.	-1
5. ●	Born again christian in new churches like Rhema, Christian Centre etc. Weergebore christen in nuwe kerke soos Rhema, Christen Sentrum, ens.	-2
6. ●	Christian - regular churchgoer in older established churches : Anglican, Methodist, Dutch Reformed, Roman Catholic etc. Christen - gereelde kerkganger in ouer gevestigde kerke : Anglikaanse, Metodiste, Nederduits Gereformeerde, Rooms Katolieke, ens.	-3
7. ●	Christian - dissatisfied with older church and interested in a new church like Rhema or Christian Centre Christen - ontevrede met ouer kerke en stel belang in 'n nuwe kerk soos Rhema of Christen Sentrum	-4
8. ●	Christian - occasional churchgoer in older established church Christen - ongereelde kerkganger in ouer gevestigde kerk	-5
9. ●	Christian - not actively church going Christen - nie aktiewe kerkganger nie	-6
●	Other christian denomination (SPECIFY) Ander christen denominasie (SPESIFISEER)	-7
●	Other religion (SPECIFY) Ander geloof (SPESIFISEER)	-8

74-

DESCRIPTION OF RELIGIOUS LIFE

BASE : ALL INFORMANTS

Q C1 WHICH ONE OF THE FOLLOWING STATEMENTS DESCRIBES YOUR RELIGIOUS LIFE NOW?

	TOTAL	MONTHLY INCOME				AGE				LANGUAGE		SEX	
		R2500	R1400-R2499	R500-R1399	R1-R499	16-24	25-34	35-49	50+	ENG/OTHER	AFR/BOTH	MALE	FEMALE
NUMBER OF INFORMANTS	501	52	161	238	50	94	107	115	185	357	144	251	250
POPULATION - 000'S	367	38	119	173	37	79	74	94	120	256	111	176	191
	%	%	%	%	%	%	%	%	%	%	%	%	%
STATEMENTS													
NOT RELIGIOUS	38 / 10.2	7 / 18.9	15 / 12.2	14 / 8.0	2 / 5.5	6 / 7.9	10 / 13.3	12 / 13.2	9 / 7.6	36 / 13.9	2 / 1.8	25 / 14.1	13 / 6.7
JEWISH	3 / 0.8	1 / 2.3	1 / -	1 / 0.4	- / -	1 / 1.0	- / -	1 / 0.9	1 / 1.2	3 / 1.2	- / -	1 / 0.3	2 / 1.3
BORN AGAIN CHARISMATIC OLDER CHURCHES - ANGLICAN/RC/METHOD.	31 / 8.8	1 / 1.9	15 / 12.2	12 / 7.2	3 / 8.3	10 / 12.7	4 / 5.8	5 / 5.2	11 / 9.5	29 / 11.2	2 / 1.9	12 / 6.8	19 / 9.9
BORN AGAIN CHRISTIAN IN PENTECOSTAL CHURCHES - FULL GOSPEL, ASSEMBLIES OF GOD	24 / 6.4	1 / 2.1	3 / 2.5	16 / 9.3	4 / 10.3	8 / 9.8	4 / 5.8	7 / 6.9	5 / 4.3	10 / 4.0	13 / 12.0	10 / 5.9	13 / 7.0
BORN AGAIN CHRISTIAN IN NEW CHURCHES - RHEMA CHRISTIAN CITY	6 / 1.6	2 / 4.4	- / -	4 / 2.3	- / -	2 / 2.9	- / -	3 / 2.8	1 / 0.6	5 / 1.9	1 / 0.5	2 / 0.9	4 / 2.1
CHRISTIAN - REGULAR CHURCHGOER IN OLD EST. CHURCHES	116 / 31.6	11 / 27.8	36 / 30.7	55 / 32.0	14 / 36.5	22 / 28.0	20 / 26.6	34 / 35.7	40 / 33.8	63 / 24.5	53 / 48.1	54 / 30.8	62 / 32.4
CHRISTIAN - DISSATISFIED WITH OLDER CHURCH AND INTERESTED IN A NEW CHURCH LIKE RHEMA	7 / 1.9	0 / 1.1	4 / 3.4	2 / 1.4	- / -	2 / 2.6	1 / 1.5	3 / 2.7	1 / 1.1	4 / 1.4	3 / 3.0	4 / 2.0	3 / 1.8
CHRISTIAN - OCCASIONAL CHURCHGOER IN OLDER EST. CHURCH	54 / 14.7	5 / 13.6	19 / 15.8	27 / 15.6	3 / 7.7	7 / 9.1	11 / 14.9	14 / 15.1	21 / 17.8	37 / 14.4	17 / 15.3	25 / 14.5	28 / 14.8
CHRISTIAN - NOT ACTIVELY CHURCH GOING	80 / 21.7	11 / 27.9	25 / 21.1	36 / 20.8	8 / 21.6	19 / 24.6	22 / 29.8	14 / 14.3	25 / 20.6	65 / 25.5	15 / 13.1	41 / 23.1	39 / 20.4
OTHER CHRISTIAN DENOMINATION	8 / 2.2	- / -	1 / 0.8	3 / 1.9	4 / 10.1	1 / 1.2	2 / 2.4	2 / 2.1	3 / 2.7	4 / 1.7	4 / 3.2	2 / 1.3	6 / 2.7
OTHER RELIGION	2 / 0.5	- / -	- / -	2 / 1.1	- / -	- / -	- / -	1 / 1.0	1 / 0.8	1 / 0.4	- / 0.3	0 / 0.2	1 / 0.8

DESCRIPTION OF RELIGIOUS LIFE

BASE : ALL INFORMANTS

Q C1 WHICH ONE OF THE FOLLOWING STATEMENTS DESCRIBES YOUR RELIGIOUS LIFE NOW?

	TOTAL	AREAS				TV VIEWING			MARITAL STATUS	
		DURBAN	PMB	TOWNS	VILL-AGES	LIGHT	MEDIUM	HEAVY	MARR-IED	SIN-GLE
NUMBER OF INFORMANTS / POPULATION	501 / 367 %	306 / 224 %	57 / 39 %	69 / 54 %	69 / 50 %	240 / 176 %	166 / 122 %	95 / 69 %	348 / 246 %	153 / 120 %
STATEMENTS										
NOT RELIGIOUS	38 / 10.2	31 / 13.8	4 / 9.3	2 / 3.8	1 / 1.8	23 / 13.3	12 / 9.5	3 / 3.6	26 / 10.7	11 / 9.3
JEWISH	3 / 0.8	3 / 1.4	–	–	–	3 / 1.7	1 / 0.6	–	1 / 0.3	2 / 1.3
BORN AGAIN CHARISMATIC OLDER CHURCHES – ANGLICAN/RC/METHOD.	31 / 8.4	24 / 10.5	2 / 5.6	2 / 3.6	3 / 6.1	17 / 9.7	8 / 6.4	6 / 8.5	13 / 5.4	17 / 14.5
BORN AGAIN CHRISTIAN IN PENTECOSTAL CHURCHES – FULL GOSPEL, ASSEMBLIES OF GOD	24 / 6.4	9 / 4.2	3 / 7.7	6 / 10.4	5 / 11.1	6 / 3.4	11 / 8.8	7 / 10.0	18 / 7.4	5 / 4.5
BORN AGAIN CHRISTIAN IN NEW CHURCHES – RHEMA CHRISTIAN CITY	6 / 1.6	5 / 2.3	1 / 1.5	–	–	4 / 2.4	1 / 0.7	1 / 0.8	3 / 1.3	3 / 2.1
CHRISTIAN – REGULAR CHURCHGOER IN OLD EST. CHURCHES	116 / 31.6	67 / 30.0	12 / 29.3	19 / 36.0	18 / 35.9	55 / 31.1	40 / 33.2	21 / 30.2	82 / 33.5	33 / 27.8
CHRISTIAN – DISSATISFIED WITH OLDER CHURCH AND INTERESTED IN A NEW CHURCH LIKE RHEMA	7 / 1.9	3 / 1.5	1 / 3.0	2 / 3.2	1 / 1.5	5 / 3.0	2 / 1.4	–	5 / 2.0	2 / 1.7
CHRISTIAN – OCCASIONAL CHURCHGOER IN OLDER EST. CHURCH	54 / 14.7	29 / 12.8	4 / 9.3	9 / 17.1	12 / 24.6	22 / 12.6	18 / 14.9	14 / 19.8	39 / 15.8	15 / 12.3
CHRISTIAN – NOT ACTIVELY CHURCH GOING	90 / 21.7	50 / 22.2	12 / 30.1	11 / 21.2	7 / 13.2	37 / 21.3	29 / 23.6	13 / 19.4	50 / 20.4	29 / 24.3
OTHER CHRISTIAN DENOMINATION	8 / 2.2	3 / 1.3	–	2 / 2.8	2 / 4.0	3 / 1.7	1 / 0.9	4 / 5.6	5 / 2.1	3 / 2.2
OTHER RELIGION	2 / 0.5	–	–	1 / 1.8	1 / 1.8	– / 0.3	–	1 / 1.9	2 / 0.8	1 / –

DATA FOR DECISIONS

MRA

DATA VIR BESLISSINGS

PROBABILITY SAMPLING

In many cases the choice of sampling method to be used is of critical importance to the validity and usefulness of the results obtained from a market research survey.

The ideal answers to most marketing problems would be obtained by asking questions to every single person in South Africa about the problem being investigated. However, this is clearly impractical from both a logistics and cost point of view. Furthermore, if the correct sampling method is used, there is no need to go to these extreme lengths to get the answers.

In general, two methods of sampling are used by South African research companies - Area stratified probability sampling and quota sampling. Quota sampling has its place in small surveys, where knowing the accuracy of the results is unimportant. However, it has major disadvantages when it is used on the majority of surveys being conducted in South Africa at present.

Three major features are inherent in Probability Sampling :

1. Only if the sample has been drawn by probability selection methods can the results of the survey be assessed within known limits of error. In other words, it's reliability can be assessed statistically. For example, if 75% of respondents use a product out of a sample of 1 000 respondents then we can say the 75% is accurate within plus or minus 2,7%.

2. Only if probability sampling is used can results be compared between two surveys. In other words a survey repeated a few months, a year, or more, after the original survey, will always give results which are comparable to the original survey.

3. The results of a probability sample can be weighted up to the total population being studied as they are representative of that population.

None of the features mentioned above can be attained by quota sampling, no matter how large the original sample was. This has major implications on the results on any survey. Using the quota sampling method means that the levels of accuracy of the results can never be known. Therefore a response of 75% of the respondents using a product can never be assessed as being within known levels of accuracy. In addition, when a quota sample is used, no two surveys can be directly comparable. A survey done a month after the original survey can not be compared to that original survey with any level of confidence in the results.

Because of the tremendous advantages of probability sampling, MRA has developed its own nation-wide dwelling unit census from which probability samples can be drawn. MRA is the only research company in South Africa to have this facility. The company rejected the use of both the voters role and the telephone directories as a source for probability sampling on major household surveys. Neither source is complete enough for the drawing of a true probability sample. Anytime an additional quota has to be put on a so-called probability sample using either of the sources it becomes a quota sample and subject to the same shortcomings previously mentioned.

Market Research Africa (Pty) Ltd./(Edms) Bpk. Research House/-gebou, 178 Fox St., Johannesburg 2001 ©
Box/Posbus 10483 Johannesburg 2000. T/A 'Merkseerch' Tel.: From 28-2863' to 28-2877 Telex: 8-3598

MARGIN OF ERROR

All sample surveys are subject to a probable margin of error. The statistical reliability of a survey where probability sampling was used can be determined and is dependent upon the size of the sample used, the unanimity of the response.

A sample survey deals with a microcosm of the total population and it is impossible to discover the exact proportion of people who act in a certain way. However, by determining the standard error of the sample it is possible to say with a pre-determined degree of accuracy, that the true proportions fall within certain limits. For example, if 600 randomly selected people are interviewed and 35% of them claim to use a certain product, then the probable margin of error would, in 95 cases out of 100, be within plus or minus 4% of this figure. In other words the true figure would lie somewhere between 31% (35% - 4%) and 39% (35% + 4%).

The next table gives the percentages which have to be added to and subtracted from any survey finding to establish the range within which the true proportion of the population will fall in 95 cases out of 100.

229.

MARGIN OF ERROR

If the margin of error given in the table below for any particular response rate is added to and subtracted from that response rate, the true finding would fall within the range of response thus obtained, in 95 cases out of 100 (at the 2-sigma level).

TABLE OF MARGIN OF ERROR AT THE 95% CONFIDENCE LEVEL

RESPONSE RATE SAMPLE SIZE	95% or 5%	90% or 10%	85% or 15%	80% or 20%	75% or 25%	70% or 30%	65% or 35%	60% or 40%	55% or 45%	50% or 50%
	%	%	%	%	%	%	%	%	%	%
50	6.2	8.5	10.1	11.3	12.2	13.0	13.5	13.9	14.1	14.1
100	4.4	6.0	7.1	8.0	8.7	9.2	9.5	9.8	9.9	10.0
150	3.6	4.9	5.8	6.5	7.1	7.5	7.8	8.0	8.1	8.2
200	3.1	4.2	5.1	5.7	6.1	6.5	6.7	6.9	7.0	7.1
300	2.5	3.5	4.1	4.6	5.0	5.3	5.5	5.7	5.7	5.8
400	2.2	3.0	3.6	4.0	4.3	4.6	4.8	4.9	5.0	5.0
500	2.0	2.6	3.2	3.6	3.8	4.0	4.2	4.4	4.4	4.4
600	1.7	2.4	3.0	3.2	3.6	3.8	4.0	4.0	4.0	4.0
800	1.6	2.2	2.6	2.8	3.0	3.2	3.4	3.4	3.6	3.6
1000	1.4	1.8	2.2	2.6	2.8	2.8	3.0	3.0	3.2	3.2
1200	1.3	1.7	2.1	2.3	2.5	2.6	2.7	2.8	2.9	2.9
1500	1.1	1.5	1.8	2.1	2.2	2.4	2.5	2.5	2.6	2.6
1800	1.0	1.4	1.7	1.9	2.0	2.1	2.2	2.3	2.3	2.4
2000	1.0	1.4	1.6	1.8	2.0	2.0	2.2	2.2	2.2	2.2
2500	0.8	1.2	1.4	1.4	1.8	1.8	1.8	2.0	2.0	2.0

BIBLIOGRAPHY

BIBLIOGRAPHY

Adorno, Theodore, Else Frenkel-Brunswick, Daniel J. Levinson and
R. Nevitt Sanford
1950   The authoritarian personality. New York: Harper.

Argyle, Michael and Benjamin Beit-Hallahmi
1975   The social psychology of religion. London:
            Routledge and Kegan Paul.

Barrett, David B. (ed.)
1982   World Christian Encyclopaedia. Nairobi: Oxford
            University Press.

Beckford, A.
1976   'New wine in new bottles: a departure from church-
            sect conceptual tradition.' Social Compass 23 (1):
            71-85.

Bekker, Leon
1982   'Two ways to God.' Sunday Tribune, 29 August.

Bellah, Robert N.
1978   'The role of preaching in a corrupt republic.'
            Christianity and Crisis 38 (20) (25 December):
            317-322.

Bird, Frederick
1979   'The pursuit of innocence: new religious movements
            and moral accountability.' Sociological Analysis
            40 (4) (Winter): 335-346.

Bosch, David J.
1981   'Evangelism: an holistic approach.' Journal of
            Theology for Southern Africa 36 (September): 43-63.

Bradfield, Cecil David
1979   'Deprivation and the emergence of neo-Pentecostalism
            in American Christianity.' South African Journal
            of Sociology 20 (September): 36-47.

Channel: a magazine devoted to the Good News
1983   1 (9) Johannesburg.

Christian, New Testament Times
1983   1 (4) (July) Durban: Durban Christian Centre.

Collier, Edwina
1982   'Born-again or fooled again.' Rand Daily Mail,
            25 November.

Conway, Flo, and Jim Siegelman
1981   Snapping: America's epidemic of sudden personality
            change. New York: Dell Publishing Company.

Copeland, Kenneth
1974   The laws of prosperity. Fort Worth: Kenneth Copeland
            Publications.

Copeland, Kenneth
1979   Welcome to the family.   Fort Worth: Kenneth Copeland
             Publications.

Cronje, F.H.J.
1980   'The influence of Pentecostalism on church unity and
             diversity.'   pp. 110-141 in W.S. Vorster (ed.),
             Church unity and diversity in the South African context.
             Pretoria: Unisa.

de Gruchy, John W.
1978   'The great evangelical reversal: South African
             reflections.'   Journal of Theology for Southern
             Africa 24 (September):   45-57.

de Gruchy, John W.
1979   The church struggle in South Africa.   Cape Town:
             David Philip.

Ecumenical Research Unit
1983   Throw yourself down: a consideration of the main
             teachings of prosperity cults.   Pretoria: The
             Ecumenical Research Unit.

Elinson, Howard
1965   'The implications of Pentecostal religion for
             intellectualism, politics and race relations.'
             American Journal of Sociology 70 (4) (January):
             403-415.

Financial Mail
1983   'The business of born-again.'   Financial Mail,
             22 July.

Gerlach, Luther, P.
1974   'Pentecostalism: revolution or counter-revolution?'
             pp. 669-699 in Irving I. Zaretsky and Mark P. Leone
             (eds.), Religious movements in contemporary America.
             Princeton: Princeton University Press.

Gibbons, Don, and James de Jarnette
1972   'Hynotic suggestibility and religious experience.'
             Journal for the Scientific Study of Religion 11:
             152-156.

Glock, Charles Y., and Rodney Stark
1973   Religion and society in tension.   USA: Rand McNally
             and Co.

Hagin, Kenneth, E.
1980a   How to write your own ticket with God.   USA: Faith
             Library Publications

Hagin, Kenneth, E.
1980b   Don't blame God.   USA: Faith Library Publications.

Hagin, Kenneth, E.
1980c   Ministering to the oppressed.   USA: Faith Library
             Publications.

Hagin, Kenneth E.
1981   Redeemed from poverty, sickness and death.   USA:
             Faith Library Publications.

Hagin, Kenneth Jnr.
1979   Unity: key to the power of the age.   USA: Faith
             Library Publications

Hagin, Kenneth Jnr.
1980   Seven hindrances to healing.   USA: Faith Library
             Publications.

Harding, Anthony
1982   'Born-again Christians pack the pews.'   Sunday Express,
             22 August.

Harding, Anthony
1982   'Return to faith in a time of turmoil.'   Sunday Express,
             5 September

Harrell, David E. Jnr.
1975   All things are possible: the healing and charismatic
             revivals in modern America.   Indiana: Indiana
             University Press.

Harrison, Michael I.
1975   'The maintenance of enthusiasm: involvement in a new
             religious movement.'   Sociological Analysis 36 (2):
             150-160.

Hine, Virginia H.
1974   'The deprivation and disorganisation theories of social
             movements.'   pp. 646-661 in Irving I. Zaretsky and
             Mark P. Leone (eds.), Religious movements in contemporary
             America.   Princeton: Princeton University Press.

Hollenweger, Walter J.
1972   The Pentecostals.   London: SCM Press.

Jackson, Gordon
1978   'South Africa's new Evangelicals: a new movement with
             new answers.'   To the Point, June 2.

Kelley, Dean M.
1977   Why conservative churches are growing.   New York:
             Harper and Row.

Lipset, Seymour M.
1966   'Extremism, political and religious.'   pp. 180-181
             in Louis Schneider (ed.), Religion, culture and society.
             New York: John Wiley and Sons.

Magliato, Joe
1981   The Wall Street Gospel.   Oregon: Harvest House
              Publishers.

Maher, Stan
1983   'This praying business.'   Sunday Tribune, 31 July.

Mansell-Pattison, E.
1974   'Ideological support for the marginal middle class:
              faith healing and glossolalia.'   pp. 418-455 in
              Irving I. Zaretsky and Mark P. Leone (eds.), Religious
              movements in contemporary America.   Princeton:
              Princeton University Press.

McDonnell, Kilian
1976   Charismatic renewal and the churches.   New York:
              Seabury Press.

McElligott, Terry
1982   Revival.   Daily News, 25 March.

McGaw, Douglas B.
1979   'Commitment and religious community: a comparison of
              a Charismatic and a mainline congregation.'   Journal
              for the Scientific Study of Religion 18 (2):   146-163

McGaw, Douglas B.
1980   'Meaning and belonging in a charismatic congregation:
              an investigation into sources of neo-Pentecostal success.'
              Review of Religious Research 21 (3) (Summer):   284-301.

Moulder, James
1981   'A ministry to white South Africans.'   South African
              Outlook (December):   186-188.

Ness, Robert C., and Ronald M. Wintrob
1980   'The emotional impact of fundamentalist religious
              participation: an empirical study of intragroup
              variation.'   American Journal of Orthopsychiatry
              50 (2) (April):   302-315.

Nipper, Arthur R.W.
1981   The key to prosperity.   South Africa: Arthur R.W.
              Nipper.

O'Dea, Thomas F.
1970   'Religion in times of social distress.'   pp. 181-190
              in William A. Sadler Jnr. (ed.), Personality and
              religion.   New York: Harper and Row.

Osteen, John
(no date)   What to do when nothing seems to work.   Houston:
              John Osteen Publications.

Photiadis, John, and William Schweiker
1970   'Attitudes toward joining authoritarian organisations
              and sectarian churches.'   Journal for the Scientific
              Study of Religion 9 (3) (Fall):   227-234.

Rokeach, Milton
1960   The open and closed mind: investigations into the
              nature of belief systems and personality systems.
              New York: Basic Books.

Sales, Stephen M.
1972   'Economic threat as a determinant of conversion rates
              in authoritarian and non-authoritarian churches.'
              Journal of Personality and Social Psychology 23:
              420-428.

Salzman, Leon
1953   'The psychology of religious and ideological conversion.'
              Psychiatry 16: 177-179.

Sider, Ronald
1979   'Evangelism and social justice.'   South African Outlook
              (July): 104-106.

Spellman, Charles M., Glen D. Baskett and D. Byrne
1971   'Manifest anxiety as a contributory factor in religious
              conversion.'   Journal of Consulting and Clinical
              Psychology 36 (2): 245-247.

Stanley G.
1973a   'Personality and attitude characteristics of fundamentalist
              university students.'   pp. 81-82 in L.B. Brown (ed.),
              Psychology and religion. Harmondsworth: Penguin.

Stanley, G.
1973b   'Personality and attitude correlates of religious
              conversion.'   pp. 345-350 in L.B. Brown (ed.), Psychology
              and religion. Harmondsworth: Penguin.

Stark, Rodney, and William S. Bainbridge
1980   'Networks of faith: interpersonal bonds and recruitment
              to cults and sects.'   American Journal of Sociology
              85 (6) (May): 1376-1395.

The Holy Bible (King James version)
              Cambridge: Cambridge University Press.

The New English Bible
1970   USA: Oxford University Press/Cambridge University
              Press.

Thompson, E.P.
1968   The making of the English working class.   Harmondsworth:
              Penguin.

Verryn, Trevor
1983   Rich Christian poor Christian: an appraisal of Rhema
              teachings.   Pretoria: Ecumenical Research Unit.

Wilson, Bryan R. (ed.)
1967   Patterns of sectarianism: organisation and ideology
              in social and religious movements. London: Heinemann.